How to Write Letters That Win

By

Unknown Author

Published by Forgotten Books 2012

PIBN 1000048840

HOW TO WRITE LETTERS THAT WIN

HOW TO BUILD BUSINESS LETTERS THAT COMMAND ATTENTION, STIR DESIRE, BRING ORDERS—HOW TO PUT THE PERSONAL TOUCH INTO A LETTER—HANDLING INQUIRIES, COMPLAINTS AND COLLECTIONS—ACTUAL LETTERS THAT HAVE BROUGHT RESULTS

247 VITAL POINTS FOR MAKING LETTERS BRING RESULTS, GATHERED OUT OF 1,200 ACTUAL LETTERS

A. W. SHAW COMPANY, LTD.

43-44, Shoe Lane, E.C.

LONDON

CONTENTS

CONTENTS

Part I

WHAT YOU CAN MAKE YOUR LETTERS DO

Read the Rules

TWO kinds of letters cross every desk.

One —paper, ink and formality —goes the way of the waste-paper basket.

The other —logical, human appeal — draws the eye, grips, sways, convinces.

One is the product of careless routine ; the other of conscious creation.

A strong letter springs from a mind's eye model, like the architect's drawing, the builder's bridge.

Make your letters magnetic —make them stand out —make them dominate each reader's morning post.

You can do it —if you will master the principles, read the rules, put yourself into the work.

CHAPTER I

The Part the Letter Plays in Business

WHAT is the most important factor in the transaction of your business ? What medium plays the greatest part in selling your goods, collecting your accounts, keeping you in touch with the other elements —concerns and individuals—that make your business possible ? Run your mind over the essentials in your every-day work and lay your finger upon the one most indispensable.

You cannot miss it. It's the business letter.

The first claim on your attention each morning after you have hung up your hat and drawn your chair to your desk is the morning's post. You run through it and you are back again in the whirl of business. It has put you in touch with the run of your own affairs, just as your morning newspaper has laid before you a mental picture of what the world did yesterday.

Now you take your turn and you dispose of each of those letters as the purposes and policy of your business dictate. Through the medium of your replies and your own letters to others you buy and sell, you give directions, counsel and advice, you cover a thousand subjects

—you direct a business policy over your own desk. And all through the medium of the business letter.

IF THERE has been one development in the last generation that has contributed more than any other to business growth it has been the development of the business letter. Letters—*right* letters—are no longer the mere stereotyped paper mediums of solicitation and acknowledgment. They are living, breathing personalities, with all the capabilities and characteristics of the men behind them.

Some forty years ago someone, somewhere, conceived the idea that human interest could be woven into a business letter, as well as into a personal message ; that a business letter, after all, *was* but a personal message and that it was possible to talk to a man a thousand miles away in the same words that you would use if he sat beside your desk.

That discovery, developed, has of itself dissolved distance and placed the inter-relationship of business men upon a basis of courtesy and intimacy that nothing else could have accomplished. And, what is more important, it has made possible the transaction of an enormous bulk of business at an insignificant fraction of what personal handling of it would have cost. Three million pounds in sales made by one house last year *entirely by post*—that is a specific example of results.

THE letter is a universal implement of business. It is the servant of every business, and of every department and phase of a business. It is an axiom of business that two men are required for any business transaction—and whenever men communicate with each other in business, the letter is the first and most common medium.

Analyse the departments and activities of your own business, and see where you now use letters—and then go on and find whether you have not overlooked some opportunity where letters could have been used.

Too many business men think that business correspondence simply consists in answering the morning's mail. As a matter of fact, that is the least and most insignificant of the uses of business letters.

THE letter can be used in the first place in all the activities of selling your goods. You can use it to sell goods directly to buyers; used rightly, the letter is in many respects a better medium than a personal representative—certainly it has all the advantages in cost. A sales letter entails no heavy travelling expenses, hotel bills, and entertainment charges; a penny stamp carries it to the length of the land. Nor does it cool its heels in the outer office and conjure methods to reach the chief within; the courtesy of the post lays it upon his desk. It follows up persistently when repeated personal calls would be impossible. It is a salesman that says no more and no less than the merchant or manufacturer desires. It makes no false representations, no verbal promises that cannot be honoured. It is the perfect servant of the user.

If you sell your goods entirely through salesmen to the trade, there never was a sales force so good that it could not get more business with the help of letters from the house. You can send letters to the consumer in order to bring him into the retailer's shop to enquire for your goods. You can write letters to your present dealers in order to arouse their interest in pushing your goods, and to new retailers in order to get them to carry your goods. You can use letters to keep in touch with your travellers, to keep them informed of your trade conditions and new selling arguments ; and the travellers themselves can be trained to keep in touch with the dealers in their districts between calls by means of letters.

If you are a manufacturer or wholesaler to the trade, the letter will find customers, both consumers and dealers, for you in remote towns where travellers cannot profitably go. If you are a retailer, you can use letters to keep your customers informed of new lines, bargains, etc. For the letter is not only a direct salesman, but it is also a supporter of personal methods of selling.

In fact, your correspondence may be serving the simplest needs of routine—the acknowledgment of orders, the notification of goods dispatched—yet a letter never goes out of your office that does not have potentialities of business getting. If you stop with the acknowledgment of the notification, you miss an opportunity. Go beyond and talk to the man. Look at your letter through his eyes, shift yourself over into his attitude, consider what you would do if you got that letter. Do that a few times, and you will soon be wondering why you didn't rub the machine finish off your correspondence long ago, take the man-to-man attitude and talk business through the post. There's a place for real letters in every business.

The business letter is the biggest opportunity for expansion that you have to-day. Employed intelligently, it will find you customers, it will sell your goods, or help your salesmen sell them, will make your name known wherever the post penetrates.

But the business-winning letter must be the product

of the most analytic thought. If it is to serve as a salesman, it must be created with all the care that you would exercise in training a salesman before you would permit him to sell your goods. If your argument is to convince, it must be planned logically ; if your description is to paint a mental picture, it must be clear ; if your appeal for action is to get results, it must be a real appeal with real inducement. You must know your readers' point of contact and aim your letters there.

––––––––––

SELLING is only one of many departments in business where letters play their part. If you sell on credit, then the letter is a necessity in securing credit information concerning new customers ; and when you come to collect your account it is the effective collection letter that brings in the money inexpensively.

No firm can do business without making some mistakes and having some complaints from customers. Nowhere are tactful and carefully constructed letters more necessary than in making adjustments and in handling complaints.

Inquiries come to your office concerning prices and goods ; orders are received, remittances are sent to you, etc.   In every case an acknowledgment is necessary ; that means a letter, and there are ways of making this letter and the penny stamp that carries it bring back manifold returns. Likewise when you are the buyer and enquirer, the remitter or complainer, again letters are required that shall not be weak and ineffective but 100 per cent. efficient. Then there are new employes to be engaged whose references are to be investigated.   In a dozen other quarters do you carry on your affairs through letters.

CHAPTER II

The Tone of a Business Letter

IF there has been one development in the last generation that has contributed more than any other to business growth, it has been the development of the business letter. Letters—right letters—are no longer the mere stereotyped paper mediums of solicitation and acknowledgment. They are living, breathing personalities, with all the capabilities and characteristics of the men behind them.

Getting this personal tone in a business letter is largely a matter of showing a personal interest in the customer and his affairs. If you are writing a sales letter, emphasize the benefit he will derive from owning the article you are offering. If it is a collection letter, make him feel that you are fair, and considerate of his difficulties—until, of course, he has shown that he deserves no consideration. In a letter answering a complaint, not only adjust the difficulty, but show your desire to satisfy him in full, and make him realise that you really value his patronage. If it is an acknowledgment of an order, put a little warmth into your thanks.

In the simpler forms of letters, such as the acknowledgment of orders, it is not difficult to show this personal interest, for there it is only a matter of dropping a few cordial words here and there in the letter. In the more complex forms, however, such as the sales letter, getting the right tone will require a special effort.

In the first place you must learn to look upon each of your customers as an individual, not as an abstract being—one of a thousand men all of whom have the same characteristics. The latter is the attitude of the old-school correspondent. He says the same thing in the same way every time he writes about a certain matter. He makes no attempt to adapt his letters to the different classes of readers. He sees men in the mass, not as individuals, and seeing them thus he cannot help making his letters formal and impersonal.

WE are not arguing here that you—the correspondent—must know all your customers personally, for that is obviously impossible in a large business concern. If it were possible for you to do this, and then if you would dictate a personal letter to each customer, you would have the ideal conditions for carrying on business correspondence. But since this ideal is unattainable, you must find a substitute for it—you must create a typical individual to whom your letters are to be written.

The first step in this process of creation is to recognise the fact that men fall into certain broad classes each of which has certain general characteristics. Then group your customers according to these classes. There are various available means for determining to which one any given customer belongs. His trade or profession, and the section of country in which he lives will give some idea. Then you may judge from his letters, or you may get information from your travelling salesmen who know him, or you may form an estimate from a study of his former dealings with your house. This information is not difficult to secure, and the added effectiveness of your letters will more than repay you for the extra trouble involved in gathering it.

Now, having placed the customer in a certain class, try to visualise a typical representative—an average man—of that class. Most public speakers single out some person, or perhaps two or three persons, in that audience, and gauge the effect of their speech on the audience by the effect on them. An editor often has in his mind one particular reader whom he knows and considers typical and at whom he writes. One publication uses such a reader as a critic, and the attitude of the other subscribers toward the magazine is judged by his attitude. Likewise, a well-known house-keeping magazine is tested out on one woman, who is, of course, unaware of the part she plays in shaping the policy of the paper. These people are selected as typical of the class for whom the speech or the magazine is intended.

So the business-letter writer who would get the personal tone in his correspondence picks out a typical representative of each class of customers. It is usually some one whom he knows personally ; and as he writes, he has this man's face before him and tests his letter by the imagined effect upon his representative.

HAVING selected your " average " man, now talk to him as if he were face to face with you in your office. Imagine him there, and then try to talk to him in the meaningless jargon of the old-style business letter. Try the old formulas, " I beg to advise," " In reply to your valued favour," and a hundred others like them. Can you imagine yourself talking to a flesh and blood man in such ridiculous language? Then don't use it in your letters. You cannot express personal interest in such stereotyped, impersonal language. Write naturally. Use words that mean something definite. Strive for an easy conversational tone.

In the beginning of the letter avoid worn-out and meaningless expressions, such as, " In reply to your esteemed favour of 12th inst. we beg to advise," or " Your valued letter of 15th ult. is at hand and in reply we would say." These strike the wrong note at the start; they can't convey any feeling of personal interest. If you want to acknowledge the receipt of a letter, do it naturally ; as, " The catalogue for which you wrote on the 10th is being sent to you to-day," or " We were sorry to learn from your letter of 7th that the goods were damaged when they reached you." Do not "advise" a man, or " beg to inform " him. Begging is not a dignified attitude among honourable business men. Avoid all such conventional phrases.

L IKEWISE, the old-fashioned, complimentary close, "Hoping to hear from you soon, we beg to remain," or " Trusting that this arrangement will be satisfactory to you, we are," is hopelessly stilted and impersonal. Many letters—one might almost say the majority—do not need a complimentary close. Finish what you have to say, and then sign your name. If you think something more is needed, make your statement carry a message of personal interest. " We shall await your reply with interest," or " We are confident that you will have no further trouble with this order," are very different in tone from the stock expressions cited above.

CHAPTER III

The Make-up of a Business Letter

THE first estimate a business man makes of an unknown correspondent is based on the appearance of his letter. A business man who is familiar with the ordinary conventional form of a letter is quick to notice any departure from the accepted standards. His first impulse upon receiving a communication of unusual shape or arrangement is to criticise. It breaks away from the routine ; it obtrudes itself upon his attention ; it attracts his notice in the same way as a peculiar suit of clothes or a house of odd design, a unique table service, or any other object of every-day familiarity and use that departs from the accustomed forms.

It is undoubtedly true that on rare occasions the effects of such changes are pleasing. But it is also true that the generally observed forms, especially of business letters, have been accepted for certain well-defined reasons after practical experimenting. He who adopts new standards should do so cautiously and for cause ; otherwise he may expect the same criticism that falls to him who adopts the unusual in dress or manner.

For practical purposes, the size of a sheet of business stationery should be approximately 8 by 11 inches ; even though it vary an inch or two, in either dimension, it should observe about these proportions. This size has been established by no single authority or group of authorities, and a correspondent may vary it as he will ; a man once wrote a message on an oyster shell, stamped it, and the postal authorities, in the course of time, delivered it to the addressee. But the standard envelope is 3½ by 6½ inches in size, and a sheet about 8 by 11 inches folds into it very conveniently and is handled more quickly and safely by the post office than smaller envelopes that may get lost in sorting ; the miscarriage of small, odd-shaped envelopes used for sending out personal cards and announcements has caused more than one social *faux pas*.

Furthermore, a sheet of these proportions is convenient to handle and to file. And as business houses generally observe the safe and sane usage, envelopes and sheets of standard size and form are preferred to the oyster-shell school of originality. For legal documents, manuscripts and other larger sheets, larger envelopes, also of standard size, are provided.

E VERY business letter should be written on business stationery—with a business letterhead. It should be written on one side of the sheet only, and should be sent out in an envelope with the name and address of the sender printed on the flap of the envelope.

A copy should be kept of every communication that leaves the office. Either a carbon copy may be made at the time the letter is written (six good copies may be made simultaneously on the average typewriting machine, although only one is usually required) or a letter-press copy should be made from the sheet after it is signed. Both forms have been accepted by the courts as legal copies of correspondence. In the average office, constant reference is made to former correspondence ; no business house can afford to ignore such a record.

Carbon copies are usually filed alphabetically either by the name of the company or individual to whom the letter is addressed ; letter-press copies must necessarily be filed chronologically, even when separate hooks for each letter of the alphabet are maintained. In either case the search through the files for a letter copy is facilitated by writing the name, address, and date of a letter at the top and in a uniform place.

———

THE date of a letter should be placed in the upper right corner of the page ; the recipient must know when the communication is sent ; it may have a bearing on other communications. The name and address of the addressee, similar to the address on the envelope, should in all cases be placed, as the formal salutation, in the upper left corner of the sheet, whether the correspondent be greeted "Dear Sir," "Dear Sirs," or "Gentlemen." Not only does this establish at once the exact individual for whom the communication is intended, but it facilitates the filing of the correspondence, both by the recipient and by the sender.

The margins of a business letter, owing to the limitations of the typewriter, are usually of variable width. The space occupied by the letterhead must, of course, determine the margin at the top of the sheet. Theoretically, the margins at the left and right should be about the same size ; practically, however, the typewriter lines will vary in length and cause an uneven edge on the right side. In printing, the use of many-sized slugs not only between words but between the letters themselves, rectifies these variations, but the typewriter is

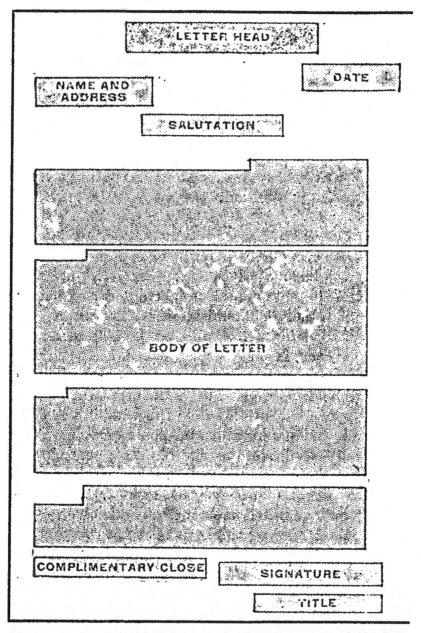

This form illustrates common errors in the arrangement of a business letter: margin at left too small; letterhead too near top of sheet; ragged margin at right; date line extending beyond margin; name and address of addressee do not balance with date line; salutation too high; paragraphs not clearly indicated; crowding at bottom of page.

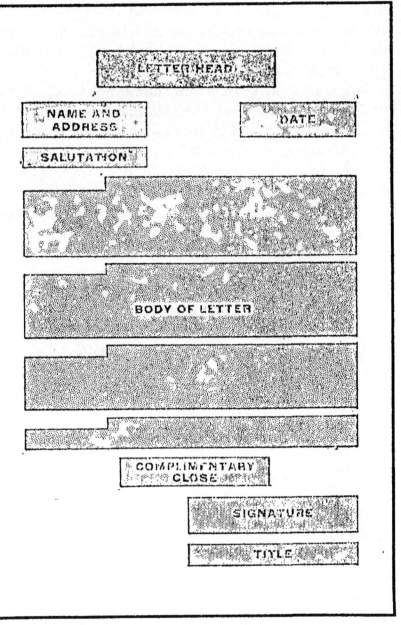

A good arrangement of a one-page business letter, showing the approved type balance: margins at top and sides uniform; paragraphs in the body may be indicated by indentations of first lines or by double or triple spacings between paragraphs. For convenience as well as economy, business letters now have usually only single spacings between lines.

not so equipped. The more even the right margin is and the more uniform it is to the left margin, the better the effect. The margin should be about one or one and a half inch in width.

The margin at the bottom should not be smaller and preferably greater than the side margins. Should it be smaller, the page will at once appear cramped for space, as the reading matter will be really running over into the margin—a typographical blunder that is as noticeable on typewritten as on printed pages.

The spacing between the lines and between the paragraphs of a business letter may vary somewhat to suit the tastes of the individual although considerations of a practical nature tend to establish a few general principles. Both for purposes of convenience and of economy, for instance, a letter should be as compact as possible, both in words and in mechanical production—it should not take up two sheets if one will serve. Hence most business letters are single spaced—only a single space of the typewriter separates one line from another. Even when a letter is short, it is advisable for purposes of uniformity, to use single spaces only.

THE first line of each paragraph is usually indented from five to fifteen points on the machine—each business house should establish exactly what this indentation shall be in order to secure uniformity in its correspondence. Instead of indenting the first line, some concerns designate the paragraphs by merely separating them by several spacings, and typewriting the first line flush or squarely upon the left margin. The best practice, however, seems to embody both of these methods, and the average business letter usually has its paragraphs separated by a spacing two or three times as great as the spacings between the lines and the first line of the paragraph is usually indented.

It is good business to have all the letters issuing from one house of similar appearance. They should be uniform typographically—in spacings, margins, forms of salutation, addressing. And no one item is more important in securing this uniformity than similarity in the colour of the typewriter ribbon. In recognition of this fact, most concerns now furnish their typists with ribbons that are bought in lots and kept in stock. Purple ribbons are perhaps the most popular, not only because the colour is bold but also because the chemical ingredients used blend well and give a smooth, durable impression on the paper.

THE address on the envelope, to which the salutation at the top of the letter should correspond either exactly or in slightly condensed form, should have the lines double-spaced ; and these lines may either be flush at the left edge or successively indented, sloping downwards towards the right.

Any radical departure from these forms should be made cautiously, especially if the various items of the address are separated from each other. The address, like a paragraph, is generally read as a unit—as a single, distinct idea. The closer the address conforms to the generally accepted forms, the more readily are the envelopes handled by the post office and with less danger of delay or loss.

Even in the matter of affixing the stamp there is a right and a wrong way. There is one best position that is attractive instead of slovenly. And it is a waste of energy even to use two halfpenny stamps when you ought to have used a single penny one.

CHAPTER IV

What a Letter Must Do—Its Elements and Contents

THERE are certain basic principles upon which every successful business letter must be built, certain invariable elements which it must contain. If it is to take the place of a salesman and do what a good salesman would do, it must follow a line of procedure in making a written sale just as a salesman does in making a verbal one. It must win for itself an audience with the man to whom it is to sell, and once that is gained it must follow the steps of the sale exactly as the salesman does when he talks face to face with his prospect, leading him gradually, tactfully through certain definite processes up to the actual signing of the order.

For this reason every sentence and paragraph that goes into one of your letters should have a reason for being there. The sole aim of a letter is to get action, and non-essentials simply detract from its directness.

It is the easiest thing in the world to write a letter that goes rambling from one topic to another without getting anywhere in particular. But the good letter writer has a definite end in mind and he goes straight to it over a definite route.

Go about writing a letter as you would preparing an important speech. There are a thousand things you might say, but only ten are vital. Think of as many as you can to begin with, then sift them to the few. Confine yourself to those points and drive them home, knowing the effect that each should have and its relation to the end you want to reach.

———

CONSIDER now the good sales-letter. It must proceed through certain steps. It must be based logically upon the principles of salesmanship. It must contain :

1. The opening, which wins the reader's attention and prompts him to go farther into the letter.

2. Description and explanation, which gain his interest by picturing the proposition in his mind.

3. Argument or proof, which creates desire for the article you have to sell by showing its value and advantages.

4. Persuasion, which draws the reader to your way of thinking by showing the adaptation of the article to his needs and his need of it now.

5. Inducement, which gives him a particular or extra reason for buying.

6. The climax, which makes it easy for the reader to order and prompts him to act at once.

These elements may be taken, in fact, not only as the basis of the successful sales-letter but of every good business letter. For a collection letter is only a form of salesmanship on paper—you are selling your man a settlement of his account. And a reply to a complaint is but another—you are selling your man satisfaction. Over the whole field of correspondence the same principle applies.

Of course these elements may not always appear in the exact order indicated, nor always in the same proportion, but they are there—they must be there if the letter is to carry the right impression to the reader's mind. A collection letter may consist largely of persuasion with a striking climax. The reply to a complaint letter may be principally explanation. The sales-letter naturally follows the outline most closely; and as it has come to play by far the largest part in business correspondence it is the sales-letter and its construction that should be given chief attention.

——————

TAKE these elements up one by one and compare them with cross-sections of a good salesman's selling talk. You will be surprised to find how closely the parallelism follows and how simple a matter it is to write a good business letter, after all, once you learn that it is merely a matter of *talking* to your man on paper.

First, you must get the attention of the reader. You may do this in a number of ways—by an opening sentence or paragraph, for instance, that arouses his curiosity, or by a striking statement that hits some one of his own problems, difficulties, or desires. This initial interest on the part of the man addressed is absolutely essential to the success of the letter. No matter how well your case may be stated in the body of the letter, or how strong your close, your efforts will be lost if the opening does not start the recipient reading.

Following this attention-winning opening, the good letter runs directly into the description and explanation, which is planned to gain the reader's interest. This part must be above all specific. Every salesman knows the value of the actual demonstration—of having his goods on the ground, so that the prospect can see and feel and understand. As a letter writer you cannot show your goods, you must depend on description. Give your man a definite idea of what you have to offer. Picture the article, its use, its advantages so vividly that it swims before his mental vision.

But the reader must have proof of your statements. Proof or argument follows logically after explanation. Its object is to create desire. It is not enough to give your prospect an idea of the nature or make-up or working principles of the thing you are selling him. You must reinforce all these by arguments, proving to him the advantage of the purchase, the saving that he will effect in his business, the increased efficiency he can attain in his work, the pleasure he will derive from the article. Proof may be presented by showing the satisfaction which the article has given to other buyers or by some novel demonstration of its quality and value.

PERSUASION, on the heels of argument, intensifies desire. Here the reader must be shown tactfully how possession of the article will bring benefit to him personally. Possibly the best kind of persuasion is the subtle suggestion which pictures to the reader the satisfaction or actual gain which ownership would bring. Argument is giving a man evidence that will prompt him to act of his own volition. Persuasion is the added influence of the salesman's or the writer's personality that brings action when the man himself hesitates.

Then another thing which the letter as well as the sales-

Dear Sir:
       We have been informed that you con-
template building a new factory, and if
so, we presume you will be in need of supplies.

       We wish to advise you that we are
headquarters for all kinds of power trans-
mitting machinery and mill supplies and
can furnish and erect entire equipments.

       Enclosed find our 1917 catalogue.
By glancing through this you can obtain
some idea of our abilities to serve you.

       If interested in these goods, we
should be glad of an opportunity to quote
you prices and we are confident they will
meet your approval.   .

       Trusting you will let us have a
share of your business and hoping we may
hear from you at an early date, we are

                     Yours faithfully,

Here is a typical sales letter, filled with stereotyped expressions and absolutely wanting in personality and real sales talk.
It follows a commonplace form of general solicitation and
would give no reader the impression that it was addressed to
him personally.

As a whole the letter is purely commentary.   It does not pro-
pose or offer one specific thing.   The only positive statement in
the entire letter is that a catalogue is enclosed.   It does not interest the reader or arouse his desire.   He has no reason for
answering it.

The opening sentence lacks the directness necessary to win
attention.   There is too much "we" and not enough "you."
Such expressions as "we notice," "no doubt" and "we desire
to inform you" are superfluous and detract from directness.

It is a mistake to suggest that the reader "glance" through
the catalogue.   He should be asked to go over it carefully.   Instead of soliciting an opportunity to quote discounts "if he is
interested," the letter should actually win his interest by play-
ing up some particular feature of quality, service or price and
showing how the goods will meet his needs.

The close is simply the mildest suggestion, inspires no action
and offers no inducement for the reader to answer.

Notice how the same matter is handled in the rewritten letter:

The opening appeals directly to the reader's needs, com-
pelling his attention.   The second paragraph wins his interest
by picturing an undesirable situation he may face and showing
him how to avoid it.

Attention won

Interest aroused by showing an understanding of the reader's needs

Beginning argument

Argument backed by proof in specific article and price cited

Explanation

Per-suasion

Prospect given something to sign

Dear Sir.

You will soon be wanting supplies for the new plant you are erecting.

And you know what a trying business supply buying is when you have to obtain your equipment from a dozen different sources. There are sure to be some parts to go back for alterations; there will be delayed shipments on some goods that will hold up all. You have probably been thinking how much quicker and easier and better you could put your plant in shape if you could get somewhere a complete equipment that would meet your needs.

That is just what we are ready to install for you at an hour's notice—a complete equipment that will meet your most exacting demands—in economy of operation—in day-in-and-day-out wearing quality.

And because we can furnish you with every item of equipment that you need, we can do it at a minimum of cost to you. The catalogue enclosed is a perfect directory of plant equipment. Please go over it very carefully. Note particularly the special prices quoted on "Star Brand" belting. This is made in our own factory from the very choicest oak tanned stock. In actual tests it has proved its ability to outwear three times over any other belting at the same price on the market. And this is just one item —just to give you an idea of the price and quality we could give you in furnishing your plant complete.

You simply cannot afford to buy a sovereign's worth of supplies until you know our price for the entire equipment. Fill up and post the enclosed specification form today. Our prices and full particulars will come by return of post.

Very truly yours,

Next comes argument to arouse his desire by showing him the trouble and money he can save by ordering a complete equipment. Proof follows in citing a specific price and article. In the close he is urged to act at once and is offered inducement in service—complete prices and particulars by return of post. And he is given something to do at once, bringing the letter to a strong ending.

man must do—offer a specific inducement. You know how the clever salesman manipulates his talking points. He always holds back till the last some extra reason why you should accept his offer. This is the part that inducement plays in the letter. And it culminates in the climax. As you hesitate, undecided whether or not to order, the shrewd salesman shoots at you one last advantage which he has held in reserve.

And, you will also recall, he follows it up immediately by placing before you an order form ready for your signature. He has learned the secret of making it easy to order. And that is what you, too, must do in your business getting letter—follow up your last inducement and your "Act to-day " by giving the man something to sign—a post card, a coupon, something that is ready to return. Make it so plain to him what he is to do that there can be no possible misunderstanding. Say it in so many words—" You do this and we will do that." Try to make your climax so direct, so strong and simple that the reader cannot resist the temptation to reply.

The New Sales Letter

EVERY new machine or process, every novel plan, scheme or principle, is a tool in the hands of to-day's success builder.

And the original thought, the paragraph or letter that abandons yesterday's formalities, that hits straight, that hews to the line of " you," is stone for to-morrow's tower of business.

Part II

ELEMENTS OF
THE BUSINESS LETTER

The Single Aim

SOME men talk without getting anywhere in particular. Aiming at nothing, they hit their mark.

And some letters go rambling from salutation to close. They are so many ink marks that take up space.

But listen to the skilled counsel making his plea. He selects his points, marshals them in order, drives them home, aiming always at one vital end—the verdict.

And the good business letter has a single design. Attention, interest, desire, are essentials en route, but they all lead to one terminal—action.

Plan your letters logically, but keep one end in view—to crystallise wants, turn desire to decision, get results, the order—now.

CHAPTER V

How to Start a Letter—Attention

MOST men *want* to read your letters. Even a busy man—a man whose daily post runs into hundreds of items—is just as anxious to read what you have to say as you are to have him.

But he can't—he simply can't.

He opens the sheet with interest, even with enthusiasm. " What's this ? " he says, " From Jones and Company—who are they ?—what's their business?—blank books, eh ?—we'll be needing some pretty soon and I'm not entirely satisfied with the last lot we bought from Smith and Company."

That's your man's attitude often enough. He's ready, willing, anxious to be favourably impressed with your sales-letter, and what does he get ?

A stereotyped opening.

A pointless proposal that probably does not contain the very information he wants.

A grovelling, beseeching, spineless superscription.

The first acts upon his interest about the same as a bucket of cold water would : the second irritates him ;

the last—if he ever gets that far—simply adds speed to the fillip with which he drops it in the adjacent waste-paper basket.

If your letters do not bring results, do not console yourself with the false belief that all sales-letters are scrapped by the clerk or boy who opens the post. Once in a hundred times—possibly. The other ninety and nine failures are due to some fault with the letter or the argument it presents.

NOT, understand me, that I claim *any* letter will give returns in *every* case, but the right sort of a letter will invariably leave the right sort of an impression. Your man may not be in the market, he may not feel able to make the immediate investment, he may be engrossed with matters of such importance as not to be able to study your proposal. But if the letter is right, it will do its work.

A bad start will kill an otherwise passable sales-letter.

What is a bad start ? I should say any opening which does not nail attention with the first phrase, which does not turn this attention to vital, personal interest.

Attention !

Study that word carefully. There are as many ways of attracting attention as there are colours in the rainbow. A few primary rules may be evolved, but these are subject to an infinite number of shadings and variations. Personal taste will determine how best to attract attention in different classes of letters ; conditions, moods and the exigencies of the moment will govern the exact colouring and tone of the individual letter. Your start should make the reader feel as if you yourself were at his desk, making your talk.

As you hope to do this by all means steer away from the stereotyped opening. You will never get a man's attention if you begin in the same old common-place way : " *I have the honour to inform you* " or " *In reply to yours of the 18th I beg to state.*" There is no particular honour involved in informing me and no reason on earth why a man should " beg to state " something I have asked him. A business man told me that he got so sick of " begging " letters that he threw them all into the waste-paper basket.

Why not say what you have to say at once ? When I write for a catalogue, for example, why should a man begin his letter in reply with a preamble like this : "*Answering your recent favour addressed to our office, we wish to state that under separate cover we are posting you a copy of our 1917 catalogue and trust you may find such a lamp as you require illustrated therein* "

Why not break right in : " *The catalogue you asked for the other day is being forwarded to you by this post and we are so confident that you will find described in it just the kind of a lamp you want that we want you to go through it very carefully.*" What's the difference ? I feel instinctively on reading the first that they are sending me that catalogue as a favour. The other gets my attention and interest because I am made to feel there *is* a lamp in that catalogue that I want.

After all, the easiest and best way to start a letter is to be perfectly natural. When a tailor answers my inquiry with "*Agreeable to your request of recent date we enclose our booklet,*" he not only fails to make a good impression, but he actually makes a bad one. He begins that way simply because he thinks formalities are necessary. But in doing so he flies wide of a good

Attention

Explanation and argument

Argument and proof

Persuasion

Clincher

Here is a sales letter that is especially good because it presents its proposition fully and clearly, and makes a strong and convincing appeal in a few paragraphs. All the elements of salesmanship are present, yet they are so cleverly interwoven that the letter stands, first of all, as a unit.

Attention is won through a combination of the two methods of opening a letter recommended in this chapter—use of the word "you" and a direct unusual statement. Another virtue of the opening is that it states a fact that the reader is forced to agree to, thus laying the basis of confidence that is so desirable in every selling transaction.

The first three paragraphs explain the offer and all are likewise full of argument. Proof of the reasonableness of the proposal is offered in the suggestion that the reader examine the ribbons himself.

There is both persuasion and inducement in paragraph four's urgent argument of money saved, and the close is a good example of how action may be prompted when you do not give the prospect anything to sign. Two instances are presented of calling attention to enclosures without breaking the continuity of the letter, and the reference to the shipping label is an especially good example of making it easy for the prospective buyer to order.

beginning because the sentence is not only stilted, but it implies that he is condescending to do me a favour.

SOME writers of success-bringing letters consider that the problem of gaining attention is solved best by use of several words, sometimes displayed in capitals or underlined, as the first paragraph of the letter, thus :

" Dear Sir :
    " BIG PROFITS FOR YOU ! "
" Dear Sir :
    " DISCHARGE TWO OF YOUR CLERKS ! "
" Dear Sir :
    " You MUST act to-day."
" Dear Sir :
    " MAY I GIVE YOU £250 ? "

This plan is based upon successful advertising practice.   It is to a sales-letter what a catch-line is to an advertisement.   You summarise the most striking feature of your proposal into the smallest possible number of words and hurl them at your prospective buyer with all the emphasis at your command.

Used with discretion, the idea is excellent. It makes the reader sit up.   The human mind is so constructed that it requires a positive and conscious mental effort to turn aside from anything which has aroused curiosity. The normal operation of the mind is to satisfy that curiosity, even though the reader's cold reason tells him that he is not likely to be interested.   An admirable example of this scheme was the letter of a magazine publisher addressed to subscribers from whom renewals of subscriptions were being solicited.   The letter opened with the single word—

    " Expired ! "

Very few of those who received that letter failed to read further to learn who, or what, had expired. Another instance is that of a collection agency. This concern had a series of form letters designed to facilitate collections, and the circular letter through which it brought the argument to the attention of possible clients opened—

"YOU DO NOT PAY YOUR BILLS PROMPTLY, SIR !"

Naturally, the man who received such a slap in the face did not toss the letter aside without learning more.

The advantage of the display line opening is that it virtually compels the reader to continue into the second paragraph of your letter. The danger is that you may arouse an interest which the rest of your communication, or the merit of your proposal, does not justify. This style of opening is like the catch-line of an advertisement or the headline of a newspaper article. The ad writer who shrieks " Prices Slaughtered " and then lists staple goods at prevailing prices misses fire. The newspaper which habitually employs lurid headlines and six-inch type to set forth the ordinary doings of a dull day has nothing in reserve when an event warranting the scare headline occurs. The method is one to use sparingly and only when other means fail.

NEXT in importance to the display-line as a means of riveting attention, stands the word, " You." Nothing is so important to a man as himself ; there is no subject on which he would rather talk—or listen. Some say this is vanity. It is not. No man ever amounted to anything who did not consider himself, his methods, plans, judgment, accomplishments, to be thoroughly

practical and worthy of emulation.   This is not smug-
ness or self-complacency.   It is the normal attitude of a
man entitled to sit at the manager's desk.   It is, if you
please, your own attitude—the attitude of self-respect.
The intelligent writer of sales-letters will employ the
word " You " with tact and discretion.   Because it is
the open sesame to every man's attention is the very
reason why it should be carefully guarded and sparingly
used for business-getting at all times.

A sales-letter is designed to lead a man to a new interest, change a man's point of view or alter his past
convictions.   Before he reads the letter he holds one of
three views :   either he never heard of your business
(in which case he must be enlightened) ;   or he is satisfied with his present goods or methods ;   or he has an
active prejudice against you.

In any case, his opinion must be respected, though
you are writing in an endeavour to alter it.

———

TO OPEN a letter with, " *You realise, of course, that
you are losing money by not buying our   * " is
to insult your prospective customer by telling him that
he is deliberately throwing away money.

"You" is the second most important word in the
vocabulary and the second oldest.   As an attention-com-
peller it is without peer, but it is a word with which one
may not take liberties.   The writer of sales-letters must
remember that he is generally addressing a stranger, and
that while a friendly, natural, man-to-man attitude is
desirable, nothing that verges upon familiarity will be
tolerated.   " You " is familiar.   It will, without doubt,
get the reader's attention.   Therefore, be sure that it
gets the right sort of attention.   When a certain eminent

surgeon was asked what part of the human body was most sensitive, he replied, "The pocket book." Even a crude appeal to the purse will win attention. Men are in business to make money. The individual to whom your sales-letter is addressed is as intent on money-getting as yourself. These, then, are points upon which we may be sure we can gain instant attention—the display line, the word " You " and the appeal to the pocket.

It is easy enough to attract attention : the rub comes when you endeavour to vitalise that attention into personal, undivided interest.

The first is a trick of words. Cry " Stop!" and every man within hearing will turn to your call. But the next word uttered must make its personal appeal or the attention gained is again lost. And attention lost is a double loss, for a man once tricked into pausing to hear something of no interest will not be tricked again.

That, I believe, is the most treacherous pitfall of the writer of sales-letters—the employment of shrewd means to gain a hearing and the failure to take advantage of the opportunity with a letter which will interest, persuade, and finally carry absolute conviction. Too many writers stop half way. They are like a fellow I knew at school—always able to get a job but never able to hold one. He told me it was because the " gilt wore off."

You have your man's attention : now for his interest !

SUGGEST that you can help the reader of your letter and you have his attention. Tell him how, and you have his interest. Prove it, and you are likely to have his order.

CHAPTER VI

How to Arouse Interest

AMONG magazine and newspaper writers the acknowledged form of successful short fiction is the "human interest story"—one dealing with primitive passions, the incidents of which are common experience. Your office boy and the director of a great railway are equally—though perhaps differently—affected by it. It deals with fundamentals. It ignores non-essentials. Human interest it is which packs the playhouse, which makes possible a halfpenny press, which sells millions of magazines and journals. Properly handled, it may be made the basis of nine-tenths of your successful sales-letters.

Human interest is a vague term; one difficult to define and even more difficult to apply to a cold commercial proposition. Perhaps the easiest and quickest way to arrive at an understanding is to cite examples taken at random from widely different industries.

Let us presume we are writing to a woman on the subject of her boy's clothing. This is a subject that lends itself readily to the display line at the opening and described in the preceding chapter—so for a sample we will use it thus :

" Dear Madam.

"*About that boy of yours.*"

At once the letter has secured attention ; of that there can be no doubt, for the boy is the most interesting subject in the world to his mother, whether he be a quiet scholarly little chap or the terror of the neighbourhood. Now what statement can we next make to turn that attention into interest and lead up to our offer. What little fact of human nature will open her mind, enlist her sympathy, gain her confidence and unconsciously bring her to that point where she will consider our offer from the right standpoint ?

" He is arriving at the age when his spirit of manliness asserts itself. You find him imitating his father's manners—he is no longer ambitious to be a policeman— he has his eye on the Premiership. Among the serious problems with him to-day is this : he is beginning to want manly cut ' grown-up ' clothes. He is no longer satisfied with ordinary boys' clothes. He wants something ' like father's.' "

While this is only a sample it contains human interest. It touches up that pathetically humorous period of transformation between childhood and youth in order to gently bring the reader to the subject of her boy's clothes from the boy's own standpoint.

WE MAY take as an example a letter written by the manufacturer of an electric motor-controlling device who wished to persuade electrical contractors to use his goods.

" *Dear Sir :*

"*I was on board H.M.S. 'Queen Adelaide' when she was hit by a Whitehead torpedo containing 200 pounds of high explosive.*

" '*A ticklish position,*' *you will say ?*

" *Not at all.   The water-tight compartments of the* ' *Queen Adelaide* ' *are controlled by Ajax Automatic Switches.   When the torpedo hit us the Ajax Automatic closed the bulkheads. I felt entirely safe and secure because I knew the Ajax would not fail.*"

Here we have war, dynamite, and sudden death as the elements of human interest.   The writer referred to a subject that had had wide publicity.   He added a bit of personal experience—gave his readers some of the inside history of an important event.

Again, a maker of eye-lotion might say :

" *Dear Sir :*

" *Have you trouble with your eyes ?*

" *Five thousand people went blind last year in Lanca- shire alone.   Over 100,000 pairs of eye-glasses were sold. Are your eyes in danger ?* "

Here we appeal to fear—a primitive passion.

The whole object of employing the human interest idea is to lead the reader naturally to the point of view from which we desire him to consider our proposal. This is important.

In the stern competition of to-day, any successful sales-plan must be given a peculiar, an individual twist. We must accentuate some point of superiority.   And then—we must bring our prospective buyer to view the proposition from that angle. This, in cases where one deals with people unfamiliar with the technicalities of our business, can be done best by the introduction of the human interest element.

———

THE problem of securing the interest of a man who understands thoroughly the general proposi- tion we have to present is somewhat more difficult.

Intimate question wins attention	Dear Sir: You believe in protecting your home from fire, do you not? But how about protecting it from the other elements?
Arouses interest	The next time it rains, your shingle roof may leak, your ceilings may be water soaked and some of the choicest and most valued contents of your home damaged beyond repair.
Explanation runs into argument	For sooner or later, shingles are bound to warp and curl, pulling out nails and allowing the rain to beat in. Furthermore, they rot quickly when obstructed and even though they may LOOK firm, they allow the water to soak through.
Argument	But it isn't necessary for you to run this risk. For at no more than what ordinary shingles cost, you can get absolute protection--in Flintoid. Here at last is a roofing that will withstand year in and year out the most severe weather conditions.
Explanation and proof	Flintoid is made of the very best of raw materials. It is laid in three layers over the entire surface. Over that goes a red coating that oxidizes after a short exposure and makes a surface solid as slate and absolutely unaffected by heat, cold or dampness.
Persuasion	Just figure up how long it has been since your roof was put on. Can you trust longer to its doubtful protective qualities? Flintoid can be laid right over the old roof, as the booklet shows. The cost includes nails and cement--and we pay the carriage.
Inducement	
Clincher	Simply fill in the dimensions of your roof on the enclosed order form, sign and post today. Yours faithfully,

This letter is a good example of the interest won and held from beginning to end. Almost every paragraph contains explanation cleverly combined with other elements, appealing strongly to rural readers. Argument begins with showing the inferiority of wooden roofs, and continues through paragraph five. Proof of quality is found in the explanation of weather effects; persuasion, in the query as to the shingle roof; inducement, in the offer to pay carriage. The closing sentence brings action.

Quality, price, service, and profit are what such a buyer looks at. Human interest can seldom be invoked to hold his attention. But there is a way—"technical interest" we will call it for convenience.

Scattered about the world there remain a few "know-it-alls" to whom technical advances are a fallacy and the march of progress a stampede to ruin. But most men are ready and eager to take advantage of every improvement—watch closely every new development in their trades. In going to a manufacturer with a new machine, a new attachment for use on his product or even a staple material, immediate attention can be gained by attracting to his notice at once your leading point of superiority and explaining it tersely, technically.

If you are writing to an electric-light man on the subject of a new incandescent lamp for use on his circuit, get right down to cases.

"*Dear Sir:*

"*An efficiency of one half watt per candle is guaranteed for the Hilight Lamps, which efficiency is maintained throughout a guaranteed life of 1,000 hours.*

"*The attached report of tests by the Electrical Testing Laboratories will give you exact, detailed and unprejudiced information on this new unit.*"

To the general public, or to anyone unfamiliar with the technicalities of the incandescent lamp business, such an appeal would be unintelligible. To men who know it is the surest as well as the most direct method of exciting interest.

The danger of an appeal to technical interest lies in the fact that we sometimes give our readers credit for more knowledge than they actually possess. Another and graver danger is that we are liable to lapse into technical jargon in dealing with everybody, instead of reserving it for the few people who understand and appreciate it.

THERE are, of course, any number of other ways to create real interest—the kind of interest that will carry the reader through your descriptive paragraphs and lead him to the favourable consideration of your proposal. An appeal to the pocket, a bit of trade news, the citing of a difficulty which is worrying him and which your product or service is designed to overcome —all of these are available.

But be sure that your appeal is to *his* interest—that you are making the right kind of a personal appeal, just as the man in the high collar tries to get the interest of his more humble working neighbour.

The common error is to ramble along on a subject which is of interest to yourself, not to your prospective customers.

"*We have just finished our fine new forty-acre factory*" may be news, but it doesn't touch a vital spot in the man who has been buying for ten years from your competitor with four acres of floor space, who gives personal attention to each order and delivers the goods promptly.

When you have your prospective customer's attention, follow your advantage by appealing to *his* interest —not by talking about yourself, your factory, and your product. "Hit him where he lives," is slang, but it has a grim significance to the writer of sales-letters.

"Hit him where he lives" and his interest will carry him through your paragraphs of description, will lead him straight to your proposal, will put him in a frame of mind to say "yes" when he reads it.

CHAPTER VII

How to Hold Interest—Explanation

YOU have attracted attention: you have won interest: now to explain your proposal. "This," says the amateur writer of sales-letters, "is a sure thing. All one has to do is to tell about the goods."

But in telling about the goods it seems that many correspondents get mental paralysis—their brains rebel and refuse the task, similar to a horse making a one-foot jump at a five-foot fence. They merely get one-fifth selling talk into the letter in trying to tell about the goods.

That's all—tell about the goods.

This sounds easy, does it not? One has but to produce a word-picture of a definite object or describe tersely a service which you offer. Yet if there is a gift more rare than that of translating a concrete article into words, it is the ability to see that article in the mind's eye. Both are necessary when one begins to "tell about the goods." Holman, in his "Talks to Salesmen," says "it takes a long time to tell something you don't know," and similarly, it takes a good many words to picture in another's mind something which you see only vaguely in your own.

The theory of successful letter-writing may be learned easily and the " tricks of the trade " assimilated at a glance, but the ability to form a mental picture and make others see it vividly by means of words is something which comes with patient labour. And it is something which cannot be taught—it must be learned.

Wrap your mind about the thing you have to sell. Analyse it—study it—finger it over with the tentacles of the brain. Concentrate upon it so long and with such singleness that the product and all its parts will swim plainly into view before your closed eyes.

Watch a man telling a story. He visualises each point and situation for his listener. You can profit by his art. Eliminate non-essentials or the points in your product which are common to all similar goods. Centre upon the details of superiority. Then draw your word-picture in a few simple, strong, definite phrases.

Easy ? The best minds in literature have staggered before that problem. It is what raises sales-letter writing and advertising to the plane of a fine art. It is the reason men possessing a high degree of literary ability are to be found to-day as business correspondents.

IN " telling about the goods," one must speak to one of two classes—people who know something about this class of product or people to whom the whole business is new and strange. In the one case, the writer aims to bring out only the points of superiority in his product ; in the other, the whole matter must be made plain.

Points of superiority in a staple goods are frequently a matter of opinion. The proprietor for whom you write must be given credit for a certain amount of parental bias. Like the cleverness and amiability of his babies, the superiority of his products may consist merely in a more or less justifiable pride in his own ability as a producer.

———

IT IS best to look at the matter from the user's standpoint always and to present it in its final relation to that user. To describe the details of manufacture and the high grade, expensive materials used in a fountain-pen is the maker's idea ; the user wants to know that this pen never leaks, is easily and quickly refilled, that it does not clog and requires no special sort of writing fluid.

Nor is it enough that these vital facts be stated—they must be put in such phrases as will attract, humour, and convince the reader.

A manufacturer of bathroom equipment says :

" *Porcelain Enamelled Ware is a perfect unity of iron and porcelain enamel—the strongest and most durable combination ever produced in a sanitary fixture, having the indestructible strength of iron with the showy elegance of fine china. Their extraordinary wearing quality is only one of the reasons why these beautiful fixtures afford more years of satisfactory service per pound of cost than any other variety of plumbing equipment in the world.*"

In some cases the points of superiority consist in high quality of raw material, exceptional grade of labour or peculiar process of manufacture. The common expressions used to qualify these points carry no conviction. "Best on earth," "above competition," "secret process of manufacture,"—such stereotyped phrases were abandoned by intelligent writers long ago.

If *Robinson Crusoe* had been written in the " best on earth " style of generalities, it would never have reached print. The earmark of a true tale or a sincere description is an unconscious emphasis on little specific points that a man can scarcely imagine, but is sure to notice as he actually lives the part or touches the goods.

ᴛAKE, for instance, so simple a tool as a tap. All one can say about it, apparently, is that it is well made, of the best steel and carefully tempered. Everybody who ever wrote a letter on these tools said the same thing in the same words, until a North of England manufacturer tried his hand. That letter was a masterpiece. In describing the goods he said : " *You could forge a first class razor from one of our taps and the razor would cut smooth and clean for the same reason that the tap does—it would have the right stuff in it.*"

He does not say that his tap is made from razor steel (which would be commonplace), but that *you could make a razor from one of his taps* (which is distinctive). And then instead of a lot of hackneyed phrases designed to convince the reader that this steel is the best on earth, he states succinctly that his tap has " the right stuff in it."

He simply takes a fresh standpoint—has the courage to use unexpected words.

The same principle applies everywhere. Avoid extravagance, vague claims, generalities, superlatives. Exaggerations gain nothing. The world to-day knows that for every high grade product there are a dozen "just as good." It may be true that yours is the best on earth, but it will take either a good presentation of that fact or a detailed explanation of at least one point of superiority to make a stranger believe it.

Sometimes whole paragraphs of description may be crystallised into a single suggestion of comparison.

"The Blank Perambulator," says one letter writter, "is as finely finished as the most expensive motor-car."

A furniture maker gives the reader a distinct impression of the quality of his goods when he says, "There is as much difference between the oak used in ordinary furniture and the selected quartersawn white oak we use in ours as there is between laundry soap and a cake of scented Pears." And still another puts a wealth of suggestion into his letter by saying : "Nothing will effectively take the place of the good old cedar chest, with its clean, sweet, pungent aroma so dear to the heart of the old-fashioned housewife."

TO EXPLAIN a new proposal to one who knows nothing of it, one must naturally begin with general statements ; also one must begin with something with which the reader is familiar. A piece of *art nouveau* jewellery, for example, is almost impossible of definite word-picturing, yet reference to the modern French school of design and allusions to a popular Parisian jeweller would call up in the reader's mind a picture which would satisfy. The object here is to stimulate the imagination rather than attempt to portray an actuality. A piece of silk might be said to resemble in tone the colourings of a rare old Japanese print, which is wholly ambiguous but leads the mind back to a vaguely exquisite memory. The result of such suggestion is almost as definite as if we show the article, while a series of superlative adjectives such as "most harmonious colouring, exquisite design, and charming ensemble" leave no other impression than one of admiration for the writer's command of words.

In any explanation, specific or general, it should be the writer's idea to so describe his goods that the reader will both understand and desire them. It is not enough to tell what you have for sale, but you must tell it in a sales-making manner. A clever outfitter never shows a scarf in the box. He takes it out and with a deft twist forms a tied knot over his finger, and the customer not only sees the scarf—its colour, weave and the play of light over the silken surface—but he sees it in its relation to himself, as it will look when worn.

A salt manufacturer carries out this idea in this manner : *"You know how ordinary table salt refuses to sift in damp weather, and when dry, cakes in the salt cellars like adamant. Our salt is always dry and flaky and it flows freely on the dampest day "*

And a maker of underwear strikes home when he says: *"Crown underwear lets your body breathe. A continuous current of fresh air passes through the holes in the fabric, cooling, cleaning and stimulating the pores of the skin."*

BUT under no circumstances, in the efforts to make your explanation of human interest, let it make an indefinite impression. Better picture your product with the exactness with which the draftsman draws a new machine, even though it does look dry and mechanical, than convey any but the actual facts, and convey them plainly. The most successful mail-order houses describe their product with the most exact and apparently prosaic details. But to give the width and length of a rug, the exact order of colours, the length of the fringe—these facts give an impression of reality and also visualise the article to the customer. Not only visualise it, but by giving the dimensions and appearance, visualise it in the place where the buyer would like to see it, on the floor in a certain spot in the home where it will fit.

CHAPTER VIII

How to Create Desire —Argument and Proof

I T IS a principle in law that a man is innocent until proved guilty. It is a principle in business that a sales-claim is false or exaggerated until it is proved conservative and true. In either event, the work of proving a case is a hard one, and calls for keen thought and a wide knowledge of human nature.

Cold, hard logic, and cold, hard facts—these alone will win.

Brag, claims, "swank," if you please, spell failure.

When you have explained your offer in a sales-letter, you must prove your words. It is not enough to express your own personal convictions ; it is not enough to say that a million of your devices have been sold ; it is not enough to give hearsay evidence or second-hand testimonials. You must prove your claims, and quickly.

Of course, many times the only way to prove that an article is all that you say and claim it is, is for me to buy it, try it, and use it. But suppose I am thinking of buying a mattress and the dealer writes to me, " *This mattress will never mat, pack, get hard or lumpy, and further, it is absolutely non-absorbent, dust proof, vermin proof, and practically indestructible.*" Now if all this is true, that is the kind of a mattress I want, and to prove to me that these claims are true the writer goes on to say, "*Remember, we sell on the complete understanding, if the mattress is not perfectly satisfactory, or better still, completely to your liking, it can be returned at our expense, and your money will be promptly refunded.*" I reason instantly that if the writer of that letter wasn't able to prove his arguments by delivering the goods as exploited, he would never dare make an offer like this. I know from experience that a plain hard-hitting talk like this means truth.

A manufacturer of "easy" chairs proves his goods are of good quality when he says :

"If I could only take you through our factory so that you could see what kind of material is put into the chairs and how it is put in—the care and pains we take to make a chair that will last a lifetime, you would not hesitate to send in your order."

The average man wants proof, first, of the values you offer. This holds good whether you are selling emery wheels or elephants. It must either be better at the same price, or priced lower, than similar goods purchased elsewhere. Even where the article for sale has no competitor, it is necessary to assure the customer, directly or indirectly, that he is getting a bit more than his money's worth.

THIS does not mean that we must talk cheapness or claim to offer extravagant values. It does not mean that we must talk price at all. It means simply that we must show the customer where he gains by the purchase.

Gain !

That word is the foundation-stone of all success in salesmanship by mail.   Show the prospect how he gains by purchasing—and not alone in money, for financial advantage is not always the keynote ; but in solid comfort, complete satisfaction, personal well-being and lasting happiness.

Show the prospective customer his gain—and prove it.

The fact that a hot-water geyser is being used by other householders in my town may be a sound argument as to the popularity of this neater, or the good work of a salesman.   But if I am looking for a heater that will save me money this argument doesn't fill my needs nor supply my demands.   However, if the man writing about heaters says, " *This heater saves you money by burning from 30% to 60% less gas than any other hot-water heater*," this line of argument fits into my ideas exactly.

An estate agent of my acquaintance sent out four letters describing the beauties of his plots of land, the select neighbourhood, the excellence of the houses sold on easy payments ; and all those letters failed.   The fifth letter was a success, brought inquiries, and developed business.   The secret of that success was in the following paragraphs :

" *You pay rent, do you not ? Suppose you applied that same cheque towards a home of your own.   You would not be paying out any more money, and at the end of a few years, instead of being the owner of a pile of musty receipts, you would be the owner of a fine house and grounds.*

" Here are the figures : prove to yourself that it can be done "

———

BUT go farther. Show the prospect he cannot lose, and prove that also. Where a proposition involves over a few shillings, the man you want to sell begins to figure the chances. He has probably been " had " (or believes he has, which is the worse for you) on a similar transaction in the past. Show him that he takes no chance with you—prove it to him.

A well-known glass company which manufactures scientific reflectors for all classes of interior lighting uses photometric curves, prepared by the most eminent independent authority, to establish its claims. Perhaps not half of those who receive this evidence are able to correctly read or understand a photometric curve, but the very fact that impartial evidence is offered as proof is enough to win the prospective customer's confidence.

Similarly, a paint manufacturer encloses a small folder with his sales letter showing how to test the purity of paint ; a clothing manufacturer explains how to distinguish all-wool goods from the half-cotton product offered in substitution ; a maker of acetylene gas lighting outfits proves the simplicity and safety of this gas—which is popularly supposed to be dangerous in the extreme—by describing how anyone may make acetylene gas with an ordinary tumbler and common clay pipe. Such proof, sometimes applied in a most indirect manner, is wholly convincing. Not the least part of its value lies in the fact that it is instructive. The reader feels that he is learning a trick of the other fellow's trade.

" Do not think because the price is small, that my cigars are made carelessly or of cheap tobacco " writes

a mail-order cigar man. " *Order a sample 100, cut open any five of them from end to end, and if the leaves are not all good long filler, I will refund your money.*"

A varnish manufacturer sends along a sample panel finished with his varnish and writes : " *Give this panel the most thorough test possible—stamp on it with your heel or hit it with a hammer. Then hold it to the light. You will find that although you have dented the wood, the varnish has not been cracked* "

A paper manufacturer is even more successful when he says, " *You can prove the excellence of our goods in a second : just tear a corner off this sheet ; then tear a corner off one of your present letterheads ; now get a magnifying glass and examine both torn edges. You find long fibres—linen threads—on ours, while on yours the fibres are short, woody.*" The man who reads this learns something new about paper. He learns how to judge it intelligently—and learning, he learns what the writer wished him to know about his product.

Another simple expedient is referring for corroboration to standard works of reference, to friends of the reader, or to specialists in any line. " *As any chemist will tell you—,*" is effective. Or we may say : " *Consult your broker as to the solid value of these securities : he may have others he would prefer to sell you, but he will not fail to endorse these.*" Nine times in ten the reader will never carry the matter farther : he accepts your statement merely because you are willing he should take disinterested advice.

There is weight, too, in a sweeping reference to one's neighbours. An umbrella maker scores when he writes : " *If you have friends in Sheffield, drop them a line and ask about Bronson umbrellas. They will tell you they have used our umbrellas for years—generations, often*

Proof wins attention

Dsar Sir:

There is a Building and Thrift Society in your town--not much larger than yours--that secured over two hundred new members last month. And secured, mind you, on the strength of business-getting circulars.

Interest

That is why this letter is as valuable to you as though it were a certified cheque. For it tells about a concise, <u>wonderfully practical</u> little book that will show you how to write the same kind of letters that brought the new members for your local Society--and how you can get this book for less than you often pay for a handful of cigars.

Argument— minimized cost

Argument —opportunity pictured

Think of the hundreds of money earners--the thrifty ambitious men and women--right in your own locality--who ought to open up a savings account that will provide for future homes. If they would only come to you and you could talk to them all personally it would be easy to secure a big proportion of them.

Argument and persuasion

Of course, you can't do this. But why not do as others are doing? Why not go to <u>them</u>? Why not put the strong advantages your Society offers before them through sincere heart-to-heart letters-- letters that breathe the same <u>enthusiasm</u> and earnestness that you would use in a personal talk?

Method explained

That is just what this book will show you how to do, because it gives you simple, practical hints on the every-day use of words--and the vital principles underlying the art of convincing writing

Explanation

Inducement

This course in business English-- costs less than a theatre ticket. 5/- brings this book to your desk--and if you do not feel that it is worth at least six times its price you can have your money back for the asking. Send us P.O. for 5/- and we will post today.

Climax

Yours very truly,

A strong, convincing letter, in which argument and proof prevail, from the opening sentence through to the clinching close.

—and always found them good. Such is the name of Bronson in his native city."

———

DIRECT and complete testimonials are also strong proof, but the use of these by patent medicine advertisers, and the numerous stories current as to the trickery and unfair means used to secure them, makes the testimonial a two-edged weapon which must be handled skilfully to be effective. A made-to-order testimonial or one in which names and addresses are omitted is prima facie evidence of insincerity—or worse.

"John Hays Smith, publisher of the 'News,' 138 West-chester Street, says : " is sincere.

" We are permitted to quote the following from a letter by Mrs. Albert Ross, president of the Woman's League, Glendale, Melton Abbey " rings true.

The name should be well-known ; the title, if any, expressed at length, the addresses given in full. Not only that, but the very words and phrases should be such as to make the testimonial stand out with separate individuality from that of the sales-letter writer. The testimonial, even a *bona-fide* one, that appears to be of a piece with the rest of your letter, as though it ran from the same fountain pen, defeats its purpose. The most successful printed testimonial that ever came under the writer's notice was one in which both the request for an expression of approval and the customer's reply were used together. This scheme could hardly be used in a letter, yet it suggests that the most important point in this whole problem of proving your claims is sincerity. ———

A LETTER which is irredeemably bad in construction, grammar, and transcription will get profitable returns if it is sincere, and those returns will be permanent. But a letter of half-truths, a letter which betrays your unbelief or evidences your effort to befog or mislead your reader, will produce nothing but trouble. It may bring results, but not the kind of results that any reputable firm wants.

Lack of sincerity in a letter does not necessarily argue dishonesty in the writer. Rather, it indicates a wrong point of view toward the trade. We form the habit of viewing our customers in the mass instead of as individuals. In the petty annoyances of daily detail, we grow impatient of their seeming stupidity, their meanness, their constant complaints, their attempts to take small advantages. And then, when we sit down to write a letter, we address a composite being having these unwelcome characteristics.

For myself, the only sure guide for writing a sincere and effective letter is to picture it as going to some shrewd, kindly, wise person whose keen insight tests every word and statement by the light of long experience.

While it is essential that every claim and statement we make be backed up and reinforced with evidence to substantiate it, there is such a thing as overdoing. Proof may be offered casually, as a matter of course, or it may be injected briefly and apparently without premeditation. A studied effort at honesty is deception, for honesty is by nature either casual or curt.

Be honest. Be frank. Be straightforward—aboveboard—guileless. From the date-line at the top of your letter to the typist's initials at the bottom, let every word, phrase, sentence, and paragraph impress your reader as being wholly and unreservedly "on the square." Follow the old rule: "When in doubt, leave out." Sign nothing you cannot substantiate.

CHAPTER IX

Persuasion

THE word " persuasion " suggests and actually involves a certain intimacy at which it is difficult to arrive in business. Before we dare employ the arts of persuasion we must know that our standing with our prospective customer is such that he will not resent our placing a paternal hand on his knee and talking to him " for his own good." When we have presented our case and adduced in support proof of every statement which is not self-evident, we may employ persuasion to gain our end.

But—as you hope for results !—employ it sparingly and with diffidence. Put into it all the ingenuous indirection that you know. Appeal to the other man's springs of action, keep yourself and your will far in the background.

Nothing is better calculated to stir the ire and call forth the contempt of a busy, self-sufficient business man than to be asked, " *Can you afford to be without this great boon another day ?—will you let your prejudice stand between you and future wealth ?* " and similar exhortation. Nothing will so quickly freeze your prospective client into glacial indifference as " *Will your share-*

holders approve of your rejecting this dividend-producing offer ? " Yet these phrases and dozens from the same box have been used and used by men whose familiarity with their own work has allowed them to become familiar with their customers.

The science of suggestion has many phases. Scientific suggestion is forceful persuasion. But forceful persuasion without suggestion lacks effectiveness. The best way to persuade a friend to take a trip in the country with you is to say, " Come on, Bill, don't stick about here all the time—come on—what's the use of wasting all your time in the city—liven up for once—come on, won't you ? "

The weak-willed man may give in to such *persuasion* —if he has no good reasons for not going. But the average man puts up his back against such tactics.

There are many men who can take you away from your business even when you ought to stay in town— and want to stay in town. But such a man will approach the matter tactfully. He will start with a sigh, "Whew ! I'll bet it is pretty in the country just now. Don't you long about this time of the year to get out and lie on the grass—to tramp through the woods—or wander along the banks of some little stream and smoke your pipe ?

" I'd just like to get on some old clothes and gather water-cress. Did you ever tramp along some fresh stream and afterwards lie under a shady tree and smoke and then take a brisk walk back home to a good country dinner ?

" I tell you, old man, it would be a great idea to knock off business and take a run up to the Glens for Saturday and Sunday—I know just exactly the place up there. Never mind business—I've got business, too—it will only be one day gone, and you do twice as much work the day after—let's be happy and have one of the good old-fashioned times."

Which man would make *you* act ?

That's persuasion scientifically applied.

First make the customer want the goods—then show him how easy it is to get them—then gently lead him over the line.

Here is a way a correspondence school uses largely the same idea :

" Think of those times when you have yearned for a future—when you have grown impatient with the barriers that seem to hold you to such a narrow sphere of life—when you hear of the career of some acquaintance whom you inwardly know is no more capable than you ! It is a matter of developed opportunity.

" Our instructions perfect you in a profession that is golden with opportunity.   It fits you for success anywhere.   Would you like to make your residence in busy cosmopolitan London ?   Or would you like to live in some quaint old southern town like Winchester ? Or a bustling northern city like Manchester ?

" The profession we will train you to will enable you to choose your own living place—there is unlimited demand for it everywhere.   Will you not let me show you how you may reach out and grasp this opportunity ? "

———

IF a touch of persuasion seems necessary to the proper rounding out of a letter, endeavour to hide it or dilute it with another ingredient.

See how cleverly this silversmith disguises his persuasion, for instance, how he suggests to me my need of such goods as he offers :

" Does your table equipment as fairly represent your taste and means and far-sighted prudence as the rest of your household furnishings ? Why not ? Your family's happiest hours are spent there. Your friends gather there. The finest associations of your household centre about the table. A sterling silver service helps to perpetuate these associations in recollection, and if your selection is a work of true art, it reflects credit upon you, through succeeding generations."

No matter how sincere you may be, and no matter how really important your offer may be to your prospect, bear always in mind that you are in his office uninvited and perhaps unwelcome and that you may not presume to the slightest intimacy.   Here, if anywhere, does the element of good breeding enter into business correspondence.

Persuasion of the exhortation type, as practised by the dominie who prefixes every phrase with "O, Brethren," is too dangerous for an ordinary mortal to attempt.

A BOVE all, don't try to persuade a man to answer your letters by assuming an attitude of injury. If a man writes to you for information about the article you have for sale, or requests the sample or booklet you offer to give away free, don't think you can make him send you money by causing him to feel that he is indebted to you for sending him what you agreed to, free of all charges.   Don't dictate, or attempt to force him to do business with you.   Any letter a man writes you because he thinks he has to isn't worth the stamp that carries it.

Here, for example, is the way one firm begins a letter which they expect to win customers :

" Did you ever have the unpleasant experience of

addressing a person upon a subject, without even being accorded the courtesy of a reply—or worse still, did you ever answer any one's questions, to the best of your ability, without receiving a word in return for your time or trouble? If you have had either one or both of these experiences, you will understand how we feel because you haven't answered our letters"

That is only the beginning of this wailing-and-gnashing-of-teeth letter. The first thing the young man who received this letter said was, "Good heavens! Look at the row these fellows are kicking up, simply because I accepted their invitation to investigate their article. I didn't find it what I wanted, so what was the use of writing?"

Antagonism is the first product of such a letter. Instead of going after a prospect as though he had committed a sin, it would have been a hundred per cent more profitable to have continued the follow-up with a letter showing that the article was what he needed.

Another correspondence school gets this idea when it wrote:

"*Nearly every man can look back—and not so far back either for most of us—and say, If I had taken that chance I would be much better off now. That is what you will say some day not far off, if you fail to consider seriously what we have offered you in our courses, for our proposal means just what I have said—a bigger earning capacity, a better position and standing, and brighter prospects in life*"

BUT there is another and subtler form in which the art of suggestion is employed, which may be used frequently and with good results. A prominent ladies' tailor used this idea effectively when he wrote:

Too
formal

Lacks
sales
value

Prompts
no action

> Dear Sir:
>
> Agreeable to your recent request for a prospectus of our school and information regarding our business courses, we wish to state that under separate cover we are posting you a copy of our latest prospectus, in which you will find a complete description of what we teach. We trust that after perusing this, you will decide to enroll with us.
>
> We shall further be pleased to give your inquiries our best attention and trusting to hear from you again, we are
>
> Yours truly,

" *I am sure, madame, that if you could see yourself in one of these costumes, you would acknowledge its perfect fit and exceptional finish.*"

Here is only a suggestion. The active persuasion is left to the imagination which, picturing a desirable result, can be counted upon to overcome the objections of the reader.

A watch manufacturer makes good use of suggestion in this way : " *You probably do not buy a watch with the idea of selling it again ; yet that is a pretty good test of value. If you want to know the standing of ' Sheerness Abbey ' watches try to buy one second-hand.*"

And even so simple an article as a patent window fastener is given a strong appeal when it is placed before the reader on the basis of suggested cause and effect in the following manner :

" Why sleep or try to sleep with your windows shut tight and awake in the morning with a dull, sick headache ? The Walker Lock will give you fresh air without sacrificing security, and you will get up refreshed and ready for a big day's work, healthy and happy.

Another case is that of a piano company, which has done a large business in the North, chiefly through sales-letters written by the head of the firm. One argument presented was :

" Please talk this over with your husband. As a business man he will be able to guide you in business matters. The choice of the instrument can be left to you safely."

————

PERSUASION that hinges upon self-interest is equally productive of results, but in the stress of much writing and in your endeavours to make each letter as strong as possible, you are prone to overdo it.

" *Can you afford to permit a competitor to gain control of this profitable line ?* " is persuasion to a merchant. " *Certainly your boy should have the best !* " is a strong appeal to a mother. On the other hand, to tell a man that he is losing money every day he hesitates, to tell a woman that she is not treating her offspring right by refusing to equip them at Jones' Emporium, is both untrue and lacking in tact.

Insurance, correspondence instruction, building and instalment propositions and other lines where the prosperity and comfort of clients is at issue, lend themselves to sale by persuasion. Commodities of daily business are best presented without it.

To sum up our ideas on the persuasive element of a business letter, the important thing is to eliminate every possible thing that will put up the reader's back. Do not give your prospect the remotest chance of hitting back, and the active rather than the passive element of suggestion should be employed.

Dear Sir:

Urges careful reading of Prospectus

You will receive under separate cover the prospectus you asked for explaining our courses in shorthand. Read this very carefully, for it will enable you to realise the value of a training in shorthand and the unique advantages which our system of instruction affords.

Interest

Your interest in the possibilities of a shorthand training is most commendable. There is a constantly growing demand for good stenographers. Every day we are asked to recommend men and women for attractive positions. And so successful have been the students of our school

Proof

wherever we have recommended them that we are now able to place practically every student who finishes our work in a well-paying position

Personality

I wish I could meet you personally so that I could show you better the practical advantages of our course. We do not merely teach--we <u>train</u> you so that you continue to develop after your work with us has been completed--so that you get 100% return on your talents.

Inducement

I am particularly anxious to get a student started in your neighbourhood. And to enable you to be that one I am going to make you an exceptional offer--a discount of 25% from the regular tuition if you act quickly. I can well afford to do this, because I know that when you have taken up our course you will be so enthusiastic about it that you will recommend it to your neighbours and friends. Considering the unusual nature of this offer, we are compelled to limit it to one week from the date of this letter, and therefore it will be necessary for you to accept at once.

Clincher

And remember the 25% discount on our £6.6.0 course means an actual saving to you of £1.11.6--the complete course for only £4.12.6.

Very truly yours.

A good reply to an inquiry, calculated to win the inquirer's personal interest and to prompt his immediate action.

CHAPTER X

Inducement

THE hardest lesson in letter-writing I ever learned was on a trip with a yeast salesman. A letter had been sent out from which there were practically no returns. Naturally the office decided the trade was in a bad way and I was sent to find out why. The first customer was a stolid baker.

"Why didn't you answer that letter we sent you last week?" I asked.

"Why should I?" he replied.

And when I got back to the office and re-read that letter I saw the point. There was no reason why anybody should have answered—there was no inducement. From that day to this no sales-letter has passed my desk without being given the test of that acid phrase, "Why should I?"

A description of goods, no matter how skilfully phrased, seldom constitutes sufficient inducement to pull a direct reply, even when this description has been cunningly worded so the prospect sees the article advertised in direct relation to himself or his business. The letter without an inducement may convince a man that the goods for sale are desirable and that they are suited to his personal needs, but it leaves a loop-hole for procrastination.

And procrastination is more than the "thief of time." It is the thief of countless orders that should be booked and filled, but aren't.

Your own experience is proof of this. You have probably determined to buy mesh underwear, a dozen magazines, a piano player and a motor car—some time. You are convinced of their good points, you know that you want them, and you have the price. All that is necessary is the proper inducement—the galvanic spark which will quicken into life this latent desire.

And so with your customers.

———

INDUCEMENTS are as various as sunsets. *Gain* is at the bottom of them all. Gain is the root of all business action. But gain is not always a matter of pounds and pence. Besides the gain in " Special price for a few days " ; the gain in the " Special reduction, if you send your dealer's name ; " and the gain in the free sample, there is always the subtle suggestion of gain in " This may change the entire course of your life ; " in " Information that may save you hours of uncertainty ; " and dozens of others that do not represent anything tangible but mean gain, just the same.

The letter that can suggest a possibility of gain so artfully that the reader is almost afraid *not* to answer for fear of missing something, is a genuine masterpiece.

The inducement of prompt and careful service is one which will always win trade ; or you may advertise a limited quantity of a certain article or style ; you may dwell on the seasonableness of the product ; you may have a real bargain—in any case, you must include an inducement which will definitely answer that cold, indifferent question, "Why should I?" And you answer it, "You will gain." Or to the question "Why shouldn't I?" you will answer, "You will lose."

A book publisher does this effectively by giving exact figures on the number of copies of certain books that he is able to supply.

"In six weeks more," he writes, "our contract with the author expires. Three times we have been forced to renew this contract, three times we have ceased all book advertising and still the orders have continued to come in so heavily that another arrangement with Mr. B—— was imperative.

"Of the 10,000 sets we have printed altogether there are now about 149 in the stock room, and 1,000 more are now going through the bindery. If you had seen the orders streaming in on our previous contracts, you would realise how quickly these 1,149 sets will be sold. While we want to go to our regular customers as far as possible, we cannot, of course, discriminate against outsiders. We are bound to fill in the orders as they come in. But I can urge you to write for your set now."

In writing the sales-letter a common error seems to be that of over-lauding the value of what is offered.

One brilliant sales-manager whose firm dealt in mine machinery and supplies won many customers by constant reference to a loose-leaf catalogue for which he issued new sheets and revised prices each week. The system was so thorough and the new sheets so valuable that many customers used it simply because it was easy to handle.

Another sales-manager tried the same inducement, using a bound catalogue of huge dimensions. He failed.

Natural expression

Dear Sir:

It is just a year since I sent you that memorable letter about the Crown Calculator. When that letter was written I had an unknown, unheard of appliance to tell you about. Today nearly 5,000 of these machines are in everyday use.

Proof

In great business offices all over the country, in shops, in factories, the Crown is saving time, money and errors in clerical labour. It is no longer an experiment. It is a proved, practical appliance which has made itself indispensable wherever it has been installed.

Argument leading to inducement

I don't know why you have been silent during these twelve months. But whatever has prevented you from trying this machine, I want to remove that obstacle now. I want to permit you to place this calculator in your office and try it even though you fully intend in advance to send it back--even indeed if I receive nothing from you but a frank opinion of it and its return at my expense.

Argument mingled with inducement

Argument and persuasion

So I am making you this offer-- an offer so fair and broad that even if you had made it yourself you could not have made the conditions fairer. It is no longer a question of whether the machine is really practical--for 5,000 responsible concerns have actually tried it--and now stand behind it. It is no longer a question of whether or not you can afford it--for under the new offer, YOU PAY FOR THE MACHINE AS IT PAYS FOR ITSELF.

Read the offer through and ask yourself if you could receive a fairer one. A shilling a day--the cost of a couple cigars--places the Crown in your office AT ONCE. The first payment of £1 enables you to put the machine into immediate money-saving money-making use. And the balance you have nearly a whole year to pay.

Clincher making ordering easy

I have attached a convenient coupon to the circular enclosed. Simply sign this coupon--enclose it in an envelope with a cheque for £1 and post it to me--AT MY RISK. Your name is enough security for me. The Crown will go forward. all carriage charges fully prepaid, as fast as the carriers can take it.

Yours very truly,

A good letter, showing strong inducement presented in a naturally expressed, man-to-man talk that wins the reader's confidence.

In both instances the catalogues were remarkable, but one was serviceable and the other clumsy—one constituted a real inducement and the other was a deterrent.

THE inducement feature of the sales-letter must always stand the most searching inquiry. To fool a customer into responding to your letter may mark you as exceptionally clever, but that customer will neither forgive nor forget if he finds it out.

For example :

A certain dictionary publisher sent broadcast an announcement stating that holders of his dictionaries who would send him the printer's imprint of the several volumes would doubtless learn something to their advantage. The bait took and those who responded by naming the imprint of the printer from whose press had issued the first edition, were immediately importuned to buy an appendix to bring the work up to date. It was a shrewd scheme—too shrewd. It may have sold books, but it certainly made enemies for that house. I know, because I was one of the victims.

Yet, while such brazen means are to be eliminated, there is a wide latitude within which the mail-salesman may work without being reduced to price slaughtering—other inducements which will pull replies from interested people and make the labour of landing the order easy. A case of this is seen in the following, written by the commercial agent of a large power company :

" *Dear Sir :—Will you kindly supply us with information as per attached form ? We are getting statistics covering the power situation in L—— and would appreciate your co-operation.*"

The form enclosed was provided with spaces for very

Dear Sir:

     You have not yet sent us YOUR subscription to SYSTEM.

     Why?

It cannot be the price--12/- --for you would gladly give many times that amount for the ideas that a single issue of SYSTEM will bring.

It cannot be the want of time--for a mere stroke of the pen would place your name on SYSTEM'S mailing list.

It cannot be you are not interested--for who ever heard of a business man who did not want his business, his efficiency, his income to GROW?

It cannot be the need of opportunity--for we have written you five letters, giving you five opportunities, and as yet you have not re-sponded to any one of them.

     So we write once again. Will you give yourself a chance to learn what SYSTEM is accom-plishing for you even while you are keeping it from your desk? We do not want to annoy you; we want to help you, and as evidence of our sincerity, make the following unusual offer:

     YOUR choice of any ONE of the remarkable series of HOW-BOOKS described in the enclosed folder!

     . And every idea in every volume is specific, practical, USABLE--written by experts. Here are correct, definite, detailed solutions for all those business problems that so long have vexed and worried you. Every book in the whole series is printed in large clear type on dull-finish book paper, richly bound in vellum de luxe. 128-172 pages, size 5 1/4" x 7 1/2"--worthy of a place on any business man's desk.

     Run your finger down the nine titles listed in the circular. Pick out the book YOU need. Mark your choice and send with a remittance for 12/- TODAY.

     We will not only send you SYSTEM for the next twelve months, but will also forward fab-solutely free, even postage prepaid, the "HOW-BOOK" that YOU choose. This is the fairest offer we know how to make. Take advantage of it NOW and thank us at your leisure.

               Yours faithfully,

An actual follow-up letter that has been very successful in getting a large number of orders. Note how, without the slight-est suggestion of apology, it condenses the arguments that have gone before then offers an inducement as a climax not only of the letter, but of the entire series.

complete information regarding the addressee's power, equipment and requirements, and placed in the commercial agent's hands exactly the facts he needed in order to make a complete and definite proposition. About 33 per cent. of the letters sent out brought back the desired information. This is an exceptional case, but it represents the extreme to which that part of a sales-letter designated as " the inducement " may be carried.

IT is not necessary to offer "something for nothing." It is not necessary to appear to be giving your man a florin for a halfpenny postage stamp. But it is necessary, ever and always, to incorporate in a sales-letter something which will answer that eternal :
" Why should I ? "
It may be simply an offer that is eminently fair and so squarely put up to you that you cannot refuse as, for instance, when a sewing machine manufacturer writes :
" *Remember, an order is simply an opportunity for the Morton to sell itself to you. There is no sale—no obligation to keep it—until you have used it in your home for 60 days and are satisfied. Just let us send it.*"
Always make the inducement seem easy to take hold of. Have nothing involved—nothing that will force the reader to doubt as to the correct thing to do. Uncertainty is the mother of inaction. Your proposition should be clear as day—" Do *this* and you get *that* "— and no matter how indefinite you leave "that," you must make "this" specific and simple. This is the real strength of the coupon in advertisements and of order-cards in circular letters. Coupons and order-cards are not so much easier to use than a short letter, but they *look* easy. They condense the procedure and show the customer exactly what to do.

CHAPTER XI

Summary and Climax—The Clincher

SUPPOSE a salesman came into your office with an article, demonstrated its qualities, proved your need of it, and its value to you, made you want it so badly that you were just reaching into your pocket to pay for it—and then, when he could have your money for the asking suppose he suddenly strapped up his sample case, said " I will be glad to tell you more about this some other time," and walked out the door.

What kind of a salesman would you call him ?

A boot manufacturer tried to sell me a pair of boots by mail. He wrote a letter that had interested me, convinced me, almost induced me to buy. Then instead of a clincher that decided me, I struck this last paragraph : " *We solicit further correspondence with you concerning our offer.*" What did I do ? I threw that letter into the waste-paper basket, and bought a pair of boots on my way home.

Any difference between the absurdly imaginary salesman in the first paragraph and the very actual letter-writer in the second ? Not a bit.

But suppose the boot manufacturer had closed by saying: "*Simply mark the size and style you want on the enclosed form, sign and post it to-day with 15/- in any convenient form and the boots will come to you at once all charges paid*" Suppose he had said that! The chances are a hundred to one he would have my money now and I would be wearing his boots.

And there you have in a nutshell the vital essential that makes or kills a sales-letter.

———

YOU are wasting time and energy when you concentrate your strength in your argument and then fail to turn desire into action. What is the use of making the "prospect" want your goods if you wind up your letter with a close that lets him feel he might as well wait a day or two ? Let him wait and the chances are that next day your competitor comes along with a letter that strikes home. Then he gets the business and your letter slides from the hold-over file into the waste-paper basket.

Make your prospect want to order, of course, but don't stop there. Make it *easy* for him to order and make him do it *now*. That is what is meant by real climax—it tells the prospect what to do and when to do it—it successfully crystallizes all that goes before into the act itself.

Every successful climax has two parts. The first consists of what we have termed persuasion and inducement —it summarises all the preceding strong points of the letter, it shows the gain that is mine in ordering, the loss that is mine by delay. It emphasises return and minimises cost. It is the paragraph that says : "*Think what you are getting—this and this and this, all for the small sum of ———, think what it means to you, to your future. And remember, you do not risk one penny. Every penny of your money will be returned to you if you are not satisfied. Why delay a single moment?"*

When he reads that, your man is *almost* ready to act. But not quite, for your climax lacks the clincher. What is he to *do* to get all the things you offer? *Tell* him. Make it so plain and so easy that he will have not a reason in the world for *not* ordering. If you don't, you haven't finished your letter, and lacking the effect of that clincher your prospect is going to lapse from his " almost ready " attitude back into indifference.

NOW how can you get him to act? Go back to the star salesman. How does *he* do it? He gives you something to sign. He lays before you an order-form complete save only for your signature. Note how easy he has made it for you to order : he does not ask that you hunt up a letterhead and draw up an order of your own. He has the order all printed and there within your easy reach.

Just apply his idea to your letter. Give the man something to sign. A post card filled out, addressed and ready to mail, a coupon that simply awaits his name— or some little easy-as-lifting-your-finger act to do that makes answering almost automatic.

There is something marvellous about the tempting power of the little blank form that awaits your name when it is rightly employed. No man likes to be coerced by another into signing anything. He balks when the tactless salesman literally shoves the order before him and attempts to force his signature. Force instantly finds the touch-button of his antagonism.

But watch the clever salesman who has learned the subtle influence of the waiting order-form itself. He

Dear Sir:

Weak and too formal

We have not had the pleasure of having received a reply to the letter we addressed to you about two weeks ago, and we pause to ask if you received that letter, as well as the catalogue which we mailed you at the same time. If so, we trust that our prices and superior quality of Princeton Piano Player have so interested you as to insure your order when you are ready to purchase. If, however, the catalogue and letter did not reach you, kindly advise us, and we will post duplicates.

Lacks interest

Apology injures and weakens appeal

We are anxious to secure your order, yet do not want to annoy you continually with a lot of stereotyped letters such as are generally sent out by factories selling their products by post--in other words we do not abruptly conclude that simply because you were kind enough to write us relative to our goods that you are under obligations to buy of us. We trust, however, that after you have gone over the matter very carefully you will decide that our Princeton Player is the best for the money, and that when you are ready to purchase, you will favour us with your order, as we know you will never have any cause to regret it.

Why should I?

More weakening apology

In the meantime, if you have no objections, we will post you now and then illustrations and descriptions of each of our new styles as we place them on the market, feeling that you will be interested in the latest, up-to-date styles, even though you may not be in an immediate need of them yourself.

Again thanking you for the inquiry, we are

Very truly yours,

This is an actual letter used as the fourth and last in a follow-up series. It is poor because not only is it entirely lacking in argument as to quality or price, but throughout it takes entirely the wrong attitude—that of a continual apology for taking the prospect's time, for annoying him, for following him up at all. This invariably places the writer in a bad position, for instead of making the reader *want* to buy, it makes him feel that his order is asked merely as a personal favour.

Now note the rewritten follow-up letter on the same proposition. Without a suggestion of apology, it goes straight to the

Dear Sir:

It is probable that the only thing
which has kept you from ordering a Prince
ton Piano Player long before this is that
-- you are still a little in doubt as
to its value
- you still hesitate to believe that
it offers positively the biggest
value that your money can purchase.

*Three con-
densed
arguments
convinc-
ingly
stated*

There are a number of ways in which
we might once and for all time remove
your doubts.
-- We might point to the 8,143 satisfied
purchasers
-- we might show you the steady stream
of orders that number more than half
a thousand each month.
-- we might show you hundred of unsolicited testimonials.

But we have a plan better by far
than any of these.

*Induce-
ment*

You are to try the Princeton Player
in your own home for thirty days--one full
month - <u>at our risk.</u>

Proof

Simply deposit the first small payment. The player will be delivered to your
home, ready for your use. Then put it to a
test as thorough - as severe - as you wish.
If the player does not more than please
and satisfy you in every particular, simply
say so and we will remove it at our expense
and refund every penny of your deposit.

If you are as thoroughly pleased as
the 8,143 others who have purchased, you
have simply to continue making your small
monthly payments.

*Persua-
sion*

Could we possibly make a fairer,
more liberal offer? Could any offer more
clearly prove our absolute faith in the
Princeton Player?

*Strong
close*

Accept this offer today. Simply
sign the enclosed deposit form, enclose
£2 and post now and the player will come
to you at once.

Yours truly,

point with argument and proof, and then offers a still stronger
inducement—a free trial of the player. Far from being apologetic, it is straightforward, strong, convincing.

places the order before you but he lets it do its own tempting. He talks not the order but the goods, not your name but your needs. And when you pick up your pen and sign your name you do so on your own initiative because you want the goods he sells.

Now the beauty of all this is that the clever salesman's methods fit perfectly into the scheme of paper salesmanship. Build up your interest, argument, persuasion and inducement and then, when you have your prospect convinced, almost ready to say " I will buy," do as the salesman does, make it easy for him to decide, literally lay a waiting order-form before him.

Refer him to your little business-getting supplement —the form or card, or coupon. Simply tell him what to do and what the result will be ; say, " You do this and we will do that." And with perfect self-assurance that whatever move he makes will be of his own choice, your man will find ordering so easy that he can't resist, he will " sign and post to-day."

———

NOTE, for example, how simple an act one firm makes ordering : " *Merely sign the last page of the booklet enclosed—pin a 15/- postal order to it— and post to-day.*"

There are two essentials to a successful clincher of this kind : it must give the reader something easy to do, and it must be clear. Virtually your offer is a contract and its terms should be so simple, its conditions so eminently fair, that the reader can find no reason for *not* accepting it.

These people exemplify the idea perfectly when they say : " *Simply pin a 15/- postal order to this letter as a deposit, and we will send the book by the return of post.*

Dear Sir:

*Statement
of fact
wins confi-
dence*

You will, of course, as a matter of convenience and economy, instal
stock racks in your new factory - racks
that will classify your supplies and make
them easily accessible.

*Explana-
tion of need*

But in addition to these advantages you will want racks that
occupy no more space than your supplies
actually demand. Every foot of space in
your factory is a fixed expense to you,
it costs you money every day year in and
year out. And every foot of space that
is wasted means actual money loss.

*Explana-
tion and
argument
showing
how need
is met*

This one feature of compactness
alone makes the Thompson steel rack superior to any other device in use for the
storage of parts and supplies. For the
Thompson is adjustable to every varying
demand. You don't have to waste a large
bin on two or three parts and stuff a
small bin to overflowing. You can adjust each bin separately to the nature
and quantity of the articles it contains,
so that parts are given not an inch more
room than they actually need. Think what
this means in money gained every day in
the year.

*Explana-
tion of ad-
vantages*

Yet as your supplies or stock
increase you will find these racks capable of unlimited expansion. You can
make additions and extensions at any point
to meet increasing requirements. Each
section is a unit and new sections fit
perfectly with the old.

*Explana-
tion of
quality*

And Thompson racks are built to
last. Constructed of the most durable
steel, they are tested to hold the heav-
iest loads, no matter how unequally placed. Once installed, they will never cost
you one penny of additional expense and
they will last a lifetime.

*Proposition
brought to
definite
point in
close and
clincher*

Arrange now to make these racks
one of the great conveniences of your
plant. Fill out and post today the enclosed post card - it will bring our representative to give you a complete estimate of your needs. This information puts
you under no obligation to buy, and it is
yours for the asking. Send the post card
by return of post.

Very truly yours,

A good letter beginning with a statement with which the prospect agrees and leading him step by step to the buying point.

Look the book over carefully. If you don't see the money's worth in almost every page, write a post card and we will return your 15/-.

" There are no restrictions, no conditions attached to this offer. It is open to every reputable business man who acts before the first edition of the book is exhausted. Pin your 15/- to the letter and post to-day "

Could anything be plainer ?   And could a man find one good sound reason for *not* accepting that offer ? Here is another :   *" Simply send 12/- with this letter and post it now—not after lunch, for things to be done after lunch are often not done at all.   But now when this letter is before you, enclose your money in it and post it to me at my risk.   And then the orders may come and the goods may go, by the hundreds—but you will be sure of your set by immediate prepaid carriage."*

Of course there are variations unnumbered to such closes.   A typewriter company uses the idea admirably when it says :

" The factory is working to the limit at this time and we are behind on orders now.   But we are going to hold the machine we have reserved for you a few days longer. After that we may have to use it to fill another order. Sign and send us the enclosed form to-day and let us place the machine where it will be of real service to you. Remember it is covered by a guarantee that protects you against disappointment.   If you don't like it, simply return it and we return your money "

———

THE simpler the order to be signed the better.   A coupon of a dozen words can often tell the whole story.   If no money is to accompany the reply, an addressed post card bearing a printed request is best of all. " Simply sign the enclosed card and drop it in the post " borders on the extreme of easy ordering.

There is something about a guarantee form, too, that coaxes the pen to its dotted line. A safety razor manufacturer who sold his goods on approval enclosed with his sales-letter a legal looking return contract that read :

ABSOLUTE GUARANTEE

" *I deposit herewith 15/6 for which please send me absolutely without further cost your ' Jellico ' Razor. It is understood that if I am not perfectly satisfied with my investment I will return the razor to you within ten days and you will refund my money in full promptly and cheerfully, cancelling the order.*"

Such a protective guarantee wins the confidence of the prospect, and this form got many a buyer because it showed him specifically that he could not lose.

A correspondence school found a winner, too, in a serially numbered coupon which it enclosed with a letter telling of a special offer to students. Each coupon read :

" *This serial coupon will be accepted as £1 in cash payment toward the tuition for our regular £4. 4. 0, twelve-weeks' course in book-keeping, if properly signed and posted within seven days following receipt of this letter.*"

But when you give your man something to sign, guard well against obscurity. It is human nature to search a wordy order form for statements with double meaning.

———

THERE never was a proposal that didn't have possibilities of a sales-climax and there never was a sales-letter that didn't have a place for a clincher. If you can't give the reader something to sign, do the next easiest thing.   Note, for example, the way the man winds up who solicits my typewriter ribbons for re-inking :

" A trial will convince you, and the sooner you send them the more you'll save.   Why not have them packed up and shipped at once ? "

A good climax is the antithesis of procrastination. It gets the reader in motion.   It tells him what to *do*.   It makes him reach for his pen, sign, seal, and stamp his order.

The clincher is the only kind of close that makes a sales-letter bring results.   Give your man something to sign or at least give him something so easy to do that he can't help doing it.   Tell him how and what to do and to do it *to-day*.   Try it and you will find your sales-letters picking up the shekels like a magnet.   The clincher's purpose is to nail down the proposition to the prospect, here and now.

The Present Task

PUT into your letter, every paragraph, your undivided and focussed force. Concentrate your thought upon it, undiluted with the worries of the past, unaffected by anticipations.

Give each problem your best. Finish it—and then forget it.

Part III

HOW TO MAKE A LETTER A PERSONAL MESSAGE

The Man-to-Man Message

WRITING letters isn't reciting formulas nor conjuring with catchwords. It is *talking* on paper.

Anyone can follow the old precedents of correspondence. Anyone can load letters with the useless phrases and expressions of antiquity. Anyone can string together custom-bound courtesies and conventionalities.

But the man who jolts himself out of the rut, who puts things straight from the shoulder, who dares to be original — makes his letters pull.

Don't stick to moss grown usages of tradition. Be natural. Be alive.

Give your letter a man-to-man message to carry and watch the result in sales.

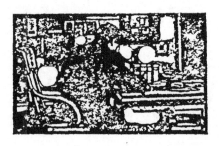

CHAPTER XII

News Value

THERE is one impression that you want your letter invariably to give—you want it to appear as a "to-day" product, a strictly live, up-to-the-minute communication from one man to another. And there is one way that you can give it this liveness better than any other—give it news value.

What the world wants and has wanted since the beginning is news. The business world is no exception. If you can tell a man something new, particularly something that has a relation to his business, you can get his attention and interest. Put the information into your letter, give it a sales-twist and you can make of it a correspondence asset.

News as used in sales-correspondence is of two kinds. You can take some live public topic—a good piece of newspaper news that you know must be familiar to the man addressed, and give it an application that will help to sell your own goods. That's one brand of sales-letter news and it makes your paper talk bristle with up-to-dateness.

Or you can tell your prospect something that is primarily of interest to him and to you. Ordinarily such news is pretty close to your own business—it is news that originates with you or with your trade, and it scores because when you approach a man tactfully about his business you wake a responsive chord.

The sources of news that you can use are limited only by the keenness of your eyesight and ingenuity. The first kind you will naturally draw mostly from daily and trade publications. Often some local event can be exploited.

A WATCH manufacturer, for example, used the idea when he wrote something like this :

"One of the last things that Commodore Peary did before sailing on the expedition that found the Pole was to purchase a ——————— *watch. Could you imagine a stronger testimonial to the* ——————— *as a perfect timekeeper under all climatic conditions ?"*

There is news, human interest, and an abundance of proof in a reference like that. It makes the letter live primarily, but it carries more conviction as to quality than could volumes of argument.

News of this kind can be pressed into service by any man who sells his goods through letters. Here is the way a retailer with a clever turn of mind made use of a local disaster :

"Dear Sir :—No doubt you read in the ' Evening News ' last Monday that the residence of Mrs. Findlay, on Chester Street, was destroyed by fire. The fire was caused by the explosion of an oil stove which Mrs. Findlay was using in her work. In attempting to extinguish the flames Mrs. Findlay was badly burned on the face and

*hands.   Everything she owned was burned and the loss
will reach £400.*

"*We simply want to say this: If Mrs. Findlay had had
a gas range this would not have happened.   A gas range
is safer, and much cheaper than an oil stove.   Now is
the time to buy your wife a gas range and make her work
a pleasure and eliminate all chances of such an accident
as befell Mrs. Findlay*"

Accounts of injuries and deaths through accidents
can be used to good advantage in accident and life
assurance letters.   Burglaries, particularly local ones,
make strong appeals in letters from locksmiths, hard-
ware dealers, burglary-insurance men, bank and safe-
deposit men.   News items regarding impure water can be
made use of by the dealer in filters.   There are a thousand opportunities for the retailer or any other man to
make his letters *live.*   Use the opportunities which
other people neglect or overlook.

Notice how cleverly this man who wants to sell a correspondence course makes use of a subject that is on the
public mind :

"*During the recent labour troubles that have thrown
the country into a turmoil, many newspapers have published statistics on the estimated number employed in the
various classes of business affected.   But nothing was
said about the mail-order business being affected.   In
this branch of business there seems to be no set backs—
it thrives under the most adverse circumstances.   The
mail-order business is one of the most profitable fields to
enter.   The mail-order spirit is in the air—we can almost
feel it.   Are you the man to stand idly by and allow the
opportunity to learn this business pass without finding
out what the mail-order business has in store for you?
It is not a hard business to break into and the remunera-*

tion is much larger than you could hope to make as a book-keeper. The course I have, etc., etc."

———

ON THE other kind of news you will have to be your own reporter. After all, it is simply a matter of telling your man something about your goods that is of newsy interest to him. It may be a new model you are putting on the market, a new service you can give the dealer or the user. Again it may be simply advice as to coming fashions or a suggestion as to the best method of handling certain goods. If it is given the news turn it gets the interest.

Here, for instance, is a newsy letter from a manufacturer of sacking to a retailer. It is good because it gives him an idea that he probably has not thought of before and, best of all, it has practical value :

" *Dear Sir :—When business is quiet and you have a few hours to spare, wouldn't it pay you to telephone every coal dealer in your town, and try to get his order for coal and coke sacks ?*

" *Next winter's supply of fuel will be largely delivered to residences during the remainder of the summer, and the coal men will need new sacks.*

" *Here is our latest catalogue, showing all patterns and sizes. Please write us if your dealer cannot supply you with whatever you want in this line."*

For the retailer who uses the post to keep in touch with his customers or for the manufacturer or wholesaler following up his trade, it is news that counts most. You need not go far to find it. Pick it out of your every-day work or your trade paper. Every housewife *wants* to know what the shops have that is new that she can use. She is glad when a grocer writes her this :

" *The first consignment of that delicious white plumed celery arrived to-day, and although it came a long way, it is just as crisp and fresh as when it left the celery beds. Please 'phone 72 Gerrard and we will be pleased to supply all your requirements at 5d. per head.*"

Advance notices of coming styles are especially good news-items for a woman, and if she gets them in a letter she will be far more impressed with the shop that writes her than she ever would through reading them in its newspaper advertising.

One store managed this matter very effectively by sending a list of names of lady customers to its Paris buyer and having style letters sent from there direct. The novelty of getting these personal letters from abroad combined with the actual news-value brought results.

WHAT you consider just common things may be news to other people. For instance, here is the way a laundryman makes news out of his methods of doing work :

" *Dear Sir :*

" *You'll often find among your new laundered collars, some that are scratched or blistered on the seam. (That is, unless we do your laundry work.) It is not a necessary evil, either. The explanation is simple. The seams of a double-fold or wing point should be evenly dampened before folding. Otherwise they blister or crack. We have a machine to dampen those seams. It must dampen evenly, for it does it with mechanical precision. So you will get no cracked collars back from us.*

" *Please 'phone Holborn 427, and your laundry will be ready for use whenever you want it* "

And here is another letter with the same idea from a bird fancier to a retailer :

" *Dear Sir :—We have just received a consignment of St. Andresburg Roller Canaries which we can offer you at a special price. These birds are of a Golden Opera Singer grade. During their course of training some birds make mistakes—others take up false notes. We call such birds St. Andresburg Rollers. They sing just as often as the first-grade birds and they all sing at night, but each bird has some slight imperfection in his song.*"

Here is an example of a letter which combines tact and effective business appeal. A prospective bride must naturally be approached upon the point of furnishing a future home with discretion and delicacy ; otherwise she will inevitably consign the appeal to the waste-paper basket or the fire with the feeling that she has been subjected to something in the nature of an impertinence. The above letter, however, is a practical and successful example of how a furnishing proposal may be made at an opportune moment without risk of offence.

" *Dear Madam :—Pray pardon me if I take the liberty in writing to you, but I hear it is an ' open secret ' that you are about to be married. May I be allowed most respectfully to offer to both of you my best wishes for your future happiness ?*

" *Another reason for my writing you now is that you will already be giving much thought to the problem of where and how to furnish. Now in this matter your interests are my interests, and if you will allow me I am sure I can be of real service to you. You want, do you not, to make a home to be proud of—a comfortable home filled with beautiful furniture carefully constructed to endure for several generations and which has cost you comparatively little to buy? Such an ideal home can only be obtained from some thoroughly respectable local firm who have everything to lose and nothing to gain by taking advantage of your inexperience, and where cheapness goes hand-in-hand with honest value and lasting workmanship.*

"Such a firm (and I say it because I know it is true) is the Blanktown* Furnishing Company, whose catalogue and Furnishing Guide I have the pleasure to enclose herewith. If you would take the precaution of paying a visit to our showrooms you would at once see for yourself what a much better home we can sell you for your money than any London house. We should really be very much obliged if you and your ' intended ' would call, using the invitation card enclosed, and compare our furniture, our prices, and our terms with those of other firms. In your interest will you do this?

Yours respectfully,

A. B. DASH."*

Just keep this matter of news-value in mind when you run through the letters that come to your desk to-morrow. Although you may never have stopped to analyse it before you will find that the man who tells you something new, the man who throws into his message some bit of live-up-to-now information—that man gets your interest.

Every business man has the opportunity of making an appeal for the consideration of his wares through the medium of news-items. The big city store is realising the value of this method of introduction and the Press cutting bureaus are benefiting as the direct result.

In the smaller towns it is possible by means of the

---

*Mr. Dash trades as the Blanktown Furnishing Co.

" Local Happenings " column in the papers to keep in touch with practically all local movements whether it is a wedding, a concert, a birth or a death ; each item can be utilised by the business man catering to the nature of the event.

Put the idea to use yourself. You will find news making your dull, dry correspondence sparkle with life. You will find it giving new pulling power to letters that have been going to the discard.

Putting the news element into a business letter does not necessarily mean introducing topics which appear in the daily or weekly newspaper. It just means putting into the communication something which you could not possibly have put in yesterday or last week. It means giving the recipient something to think about that would not have been thought about yesterday by any of your rivals.

Human Interest

THE great result is only the fusion of many small perfections. But all the right elements of a good letter make only conglomerate, unless they be fused in the fire of universal living. They fall short, until they touch the common ground of your day's work and mine.

CHAPTER XIII

Personality

YOU may have a proposal that speaks for itself, but if your salesman has a colourless personality, you might as well entrust your message to a straw man for all the good such a pale individual will do.

And it is the same in the sales-letter. If you expect to magnetise your prospect's money you must put a personal touch into your letters—not egotism, but your own honest, personal conviction, interwoven so thoroughly into your customer's personality that he feels that you understand him and that he understands you.

This is the subtle effect of successful letter-personality. It unties the wallet strings where the custom-made letter goes into the basket. It creates confidence where exaggeration breeds distrust. It gets the business where the cold, serious, matter-of-fact communication falls on deaf ears. And this is true because the letter with a personality is "different." It stands out from its stereotyped companions like a strong man in a crowd.

Letters that really have a personality are order-getters because of the two elements that are woven into them—the man-to-man attitude and originality of thought and expression. And these elements are found in every part of the letter—salutation, body, close, signature and postscript.

IT SHOULD be remembered, however, in this matter of approach, that sales-letters are distinctly of two kinds—the unsolicited letter and the reply to an enquiry. In the first you must announce yourself and win your own audience ; in the second you come at the buyer's invitation.

Naturally the first situation demands certain preliminaries—winning the reader's attention and interest—before you can get down to a business proposal. In the other instance you can glide over the prelude and make your offer at once.

But even though you are approaching a man for the first time, there is no reason why you cannot take the man-to-man attitude. What you want is his interest, and there is no surer way of getting it than talking to him about himself.

Look at your proposition from his point of view. Talk about the things he is interested in. Talk to him in his own words, his phrases. Express your ideas as he would. Make your letter a personal talk, full of life and action.

If you are trying to sell a man a pair of boots, don't talk about *your* boots until you have mentioned *his*.

NOTICE, too, how a manufacturer of motor-cars gets your attention from the start when he writes this way :

" Dear Sir :

" I wonder how near your ideas and mine would agree

in the selection of a runabout car, and if a car that I
would build for my own use would suit you. Every
year I build a car for myself—not because I wear out a
car in one year's time, but because I am always able to
sell my last year's car to a business firm here for little
less than it cost me.

"I built a new runabout car this year, which was
finished a little over two weeks ago, and I used it for
just one day when a friend offered me £20 more for it
than the regular price, and I let him have it.

" As this car took so well and everyone seemed to like
it so much, I immediately arranged to get out a number
of special jobs under the same specifications, and they
are now nearing completion. One I am going to use
myself, and I am going to give you an opportunity to
get one of the others."

Thus the proposal goes swinging along naturally to
so strong a close that I must answer the letter if I am
in the market for a car at all. He compels my interest,
excites my attention, and inspires a quick appreciation
of what he has to sell, by talking to me as if I were in
his office.

Of course, this man-to-man element of the letter must
be qualified to co-ordinate with the necessary conditions. You wouldn't write Bill Green, of Camberwell, the
same kind of letter that you prepared for J. C. Chester-
ton, of the Manor, Ashford. The letter which would
appeal to one man might very well annoy a man of
another calibre. The class of trade, first, and the manner
of prospective customer, second, must be weighed in the
writer's mind. In some businesses it is a good thing
to put " snap " into a letter ; in others, the first thing
to be avoided is the possibility of offending the suscepti-
bilities of prospective customers, more particularly those

customers who are apt to regard all trader's epistles with suspicion.

Don't run to the other extreme and employ language savouring of abasement. Almost any business letter in the world can, by a few touches, be made adaptable to the capacity of a working man or the culture and breeding of an aristocrat. Avoid suggestion of familiarity when dealing with a good class of buyer, but do not allow this precaution to stultify your selling arguments. It is not necessary and it is not good business.

———

THE second element of the personality letter—unconventional expression—usually follows if the writer really establishes his man-to-man relationship. But there are certain divisions in the letter where positive efforts must be made to avoid a slavish following of custom.

Particularly is this true when an enquiry solicits your reply. State your case from the start and, as you hope and strive to be natural, avoid the old formalities.

The average introduction with its " We beg " and " Pursuant to your request " is as useless as a third leg. Such expressions as " Enclosed herewith " take up the reader's time, detract from the main idea, and are absolutely foolish. You might just as well attach stickers, saying inanely, " This is an envelope " and " This is a sheet of paper."

If you ask a salesman for prices on his best hurdy-gurdy or what-not, it isn't likely that he would clear his throat, hitch up his trousers, and launch into a seventeenth century prelude. Of course he wouldn't. He would snap out something like this, and skirmish for a sale : " We have three styles of hurdy-gurdys, one at

Dear Sir:

Use of worn out figure

Opportunity comes to a man's door only once. He must be prepared when it knocks at his door, and answer ready; otherwise he is largely a failure; a drudge, trudging along daily on a mere pittance, awaiting the end, with no one but himself to blame. He did not grasp his opportunity.

Too general

Get out of the rut and into a field of greater knowledge, and thus be prepared to command, yes even insure a larger income. Business men are coming to recognise the value of a better knowledge of existing conditions, of organisation and systematisation. The factory expert may safely without fear of contradiction be said to be the Business Adviser of today. He assists in the organising of a business, and much if not the greater part of the success of the manufacturer must be attributed to the wisdom and the business foresight of the accountant.

Directness entirely lacking

No explanation or argument

But it is no longer necessary for you to depend upon an outsider for help in organising and conducting your business. Here is your opportunity to become an expert at a nominal cost. Fill out your order and get our book just published on "Factory Organisation". This book has been completely rewritten giving you the latest and most up-to-day work extant.

Offer not clear

Weak close

Our prospectus fully explains the scope of the work and qualifications of the writer. Any further information desired will be cheerfully given on request. Awaiting the courtesy of a reply, we are

Very truly yours,

Here is a letter that is full of generalities and so lacking in personality that it entirely misses the individual appeal. The proposition offered is not mentioned until the third paragraph and then in an incidental way.

Note how the same book proposition is handled in the rewritten letter opposite—a letter as personal as a call over the phone. In this second sheet, proverbs and axioms are displaced by reasons why the chance to buy is worth real cash to the particular reader every hour of his factory day. He is offered a particular proved opportunity, not general disserta-

<table>
<tr><td>

Exact place and date

Extremely personal opening wins confidence

Explanation

Reason for offer

Argument

Persuasion and inducement

Clincher

</td><td>

Mr. Page's Office,
Tuesday, January tenth.

Dear Sir:

This morning I received from our printers some news that I feel certain will be of interest to you. And because I feel that this is a matter of unusual importance I am writing today to you and a few more of our oldest friends, so that I may hear from you and have the benefit of your opinion before any public announcement is made.

I will receive from our printers Thursday a few advance copies of C. P. Watson's "Factory Organization"-- a business book that I honestly believe will save you more <u>real sovereigns</u> than any other book in print.

We have issued no printed matter about "Factory Organization." But even a volume of printed matter could not show you its value as will the book itself. So I want to send you the book. I do not expect you to buy it blindly. I merely want you to look it over AT MY RISK and give me your frank opinion of it.

You would willingly risk a dozen times 10/- for a single plan that would reduce your factory costs alone. Yet this book contains 22 money saving plans that will reduce expenses throughout your whole business - plans of hiring and handling employees - plans that will check every leak and waste in your factory and office. And I do not ask you to risk one single penny to secure them.

Merely send for the book on approval. The 10/- you forward will not be regarded as a remittance but as a deposit. And then, if any single chapter alone is not worth £1 cash to you, I will not only send you my cheque for 10/- but I will remit you in all 10/6 to pay you in addition for your postage and trouble in looking over the book.

Merely pin a 10/- postal order to this letter - post tonight if possible - and use the envelope enclosed.

Yours very truly,

</td></tr>
</table>

tion. This contrast illustrates the possibilities of the use of the personal element.

so much, another at this much," and so on. The salesman is interested in sales and so are you. Why not take
a lesson from him, then, and chop off the hackneyed
preface ? What is the sense of obscuring the real issue
by a lengthy prelude, useless apology, a request to write,
or begging for permission to advise ? Get down to bed-
rock and catch your prospect's attention from the start.

Note how this manufacturer goes straight to the
point in his opening :

" *Dear Sir :*

" *Your goods may leave the factory in the best of condition. But how do they reach their destination ? Any
goods station is likely to be over-crowded any day, and
open platforms and wharves piled high with freight.
Your goods are not favoured—they are just as likely to
be left outside as any. And a sudden rain may absolutely ruin them.*

" *Why not insure your shipments against rain, snow,
fog—against rust or warp or mildew. You can do it
absolutely with Andrews' Waterproof Wrapping.*

" *Andrews' Waterproof is made of three things : heavy
tough paper, perfect water-proofing, and reinforcing
cloth, giving extra toughness and strength. No matter
how awkward or irregular the shape of your product,
sharp corners or projections will not poke through. And
your goods will reach their destination as dry and sound
as when they left your shipping department.*"

Like a good salesman, this writer launched into his
subject without prelude or apology.

———

ORIGINALITY of thought and expression is really
shown in the body of the letter more than in the
salutation and close, for there the opportunities are

almost limitless. For instance, observe the stilted style of this tiresome long drawn-out sentence :

"Our connections are such as to make it possible for you to place your order with us right here in the City, where we can show you the goods and demonstrate the efficiency of our cars, and we hope that just as soon as you receive the catalogue you will look it over carefully and make it a point to call at our sales-room which is connected with our general offices, and give us an opportunity to show you what our cars will do "

And then turn to the refreshing ease of expression in this from a local tailor :

"Do you know that Henry has been cutting clothes for some of London's best-dressed men for the last ten years and that many of our old customers run in from out of town just to get that perfection of fit that they know only Henry can give them ? This is just an indication of the confidence men of taste have in our ability to give comfort and satisfaction "

Here the writer has even referred to his cutter by *name*. The ordinary writer, if he mentioned the cutter at all, would have spoken of him simply as an employé.

B UT this is not all there is to a letter. A writer who has injected personality into his salutation and half-way through his letter ends in some such trite phrase as, *"Hoping to hear from you by return of post, we are "* is as bad as the correspondent who uses stereotyped expressions throughout. Both blunt their effect on the prospect.

The closing paragraph should force the prospect into action—not put him to sleep with such hackneyed expressions as " trusting we shall hear from you " and

" begging to remain." Such conventional baggage only loads down a letter and means nothing. The prospect knows that you " hope " for his business and " trust " he will answer your letter.

————

IF your communication demands a distinct close, say something new, typical of life, as, for instance :

" *Sign and post the order now, before it slips your mind.*"

" *Just say the word and the samples are yours* "

" *Can you afford to overlook this when it means pounds to you ?* "

Millions of unread letters are tossed to the waste-paper basket because they lack personality. From beginning to end they look alike. They " beg " this and " trust " that. It's " we do " and " you don't " until the reader is as bored as you are with your neighbour's one-record talking machine. Successful correspondents are learning that hackneyed salutations and strained complimentary closes are lost on the prospect, that it is, above all, the man-to-man element—the office talk on paper—that gets the orders.

————

DESOLUTION to buy is a whetted razor edge. Don't overstrop it; don't hit it with a brick. When it's ripe *put it to work !*

CHAPTER XIV

The "You" Element

YOU would probably leap up in burning wrath if, to-morrow, you could see your sales-letters kindling a hundred morning fires. At least you would want to know why your sales-letters interest only the man who empties the waste-paper basket. You might bring your correspondents to the carpet, you might question and you might threaten, but it is a ten-to-one shot that they couldn't answer when you had done.

If you are to solve the most perplexing and yet obvious fault of your sales-letters, you must sit down and pick apart your paper salesmen. As you analyse your correspondence you will be impressed with one fact—that there is too much " we " in the beginning of the sales-missive. If you push your investigation into the body of your letters, underscoring each " we " as you come to it, you will find that the writer has literally peppered his story with the objectionable word. There is the answer to your question.

From beginning to end, the average letter consists of, " *We* " have " so and so " to offer ; " *We* " contemplate

this, and " *We* " intend to do that. But what do *I* care
about what " *We* " do ? How are *my* interests affected
by a statement regarding " *ours* " ? The closest thing
to you, is " *you* " The never-ending source of attraction
and concern to me is " *me* "

And thus the correspondent misses a hearing because
he begins talking about himself instead of " you." For
example, a clothier writes me a letter : " *We are showing the most attractive line of spring and summer woollens
in the city. The cut of every garment is the latest in
style.*"

NOW that kind of a letter hasn't told me what I
wanted to know. The fact that they are showing
the woollens doesn't particularly interest me. They
may have the most attractive line in the city. What I
care about is, what is in this for me ? How will it affect
my bank balance ?

But if they had written : " *Mr. Smith, you spend £3
more for a suit of clothes than you should. How can we
prove it ? By making you just as stylish and as wearable
a suit for £4 as you have been paying £7 for. You will
look better and feel better in the clothes, and at the same
time you will be saving money.*"

If they had said this—ah ! that would have been a
different matter. For here is a letter that gets as close
to me as my own desk, that touches my pocketbook, my
business instinct.

Again, a manufacturer writes me to-day : " *We have
perfected and are now prepared to supply our new,
patent-lined, double-rimmed, rust-proof, excelsior gas
burner—the peer of them all.*"

When I receive that letter how does it affect my cost
of production ? I hold no stock in the gas burner indus-

try. He might as well announce the discovery of a new mud puddle in Lombard Street so far as my interests are concerned.

But suppose he had said : "*Mr. Gas Burner, you spend 10/- a month more for gas light than you should, and yet in spite of this waste you are not getting the brilliant illumination you are paying for. I can cut your gas bills in two, give you better, clearer, brighter light, and save you 10/- a month. And the whole outlay to you will be simply the price of one of our new gas burners*"

Suppose the writer had said that ? It would have been somewhat different, and I probably would have hurried to the letter-box with a money order. Forget yourself and talk about the other man's profits, needs, desires. Look at your proposition from his point of view and he will readily see it from yours.

DON'T begin your letter and every other sentence with "We." You may be the ruling power in your own world, but your reader doesn't know it. To himself he is the king of his own little kingdom. He has so many things to think about, he isn't interested in what you are doing. And yet he is the man you must get close to if you expect to get any of his money. He is interested only when he is sure of getting some money himself. I at once became interested when I received this letter :

"*Mr. Retailer :*

"*Why is it that you—the retailer—are compelled to lose more good hard cash through bad debts than any other man in business ?*

"*Every month you have to charge up to bad debts, scores of good fat accounts that debtors refuse to pay.*

Dear Sir:

Accept our thanks for your favour just received. We are glad of this opportunity to forward you a catalogue showing the styles which we carry in our Stock Room ready for immediate use.

Formal—
"our"
stock

Of course it is impossible to show all the styles which we make. The illustrations shown, simply represent some of the season's best sellers as selected by the leading retailers from our two hundred and fifty styles designed by our selling force.

"Our"
styles

Our boots are correct in every sense of the word. Our oxfords possess superior fitting qualities. They do not gap at the ankle; they fit close and do not slip at the heel; they are the coolest boot for summer. We have them in Green, Red, Tan, Black and Patent.

"Our"
qualities

Our Guarantee is something that is of vital importance to you if you care to be assured of full value for your money spent.

"Our"
guarantee

We can make any style required if you fail to find illustrated in our catalogue just the boot you desire at the present time. We will forward the boots prepaid upon receipt of your order with price and will strive to serve you in a most satisfactory manner.

"Our"
catalogue

Yours very truly,

Nothing robs a letter of directness so much as a lack of the "you" element. Here is an actual letter which illustrates particularly well an absence of direct appeal because of this fault.

This man tries to sell a pair of boots, not by talking about the prospect and his needs, but about himself and his product. Note the prevalence of "our" and "we" in every paragraph. Half the words are mere machinery of this antique variety, through which "we accept, are glad, make, strive," and so on. The real meat—the specific words that catch the eye—could be compressed into two short paragraphs.

Then note how the same proposition is handled in the rewritten letter. The dealer comes over to the customer's side, just as a clever salesman would, and turns in to help him "get a fit." "That's right," he says, "a poor fit is a real calamity. What you want is this and this and this—and here is a stock of boots among which you'll find those very things." So the entire letter shows an understanding of "your" boot

<table>
<tr><td>

"Your"
boot
troubles

"Your"
wants

"Your"
comfort
assured

"Your"
wants
supplied

"Your"
choice

"Your"
oppor-
tunity
grasped

</td><td>

Dear Sir:

What is more uncomfortable and aggravating than an ill-fitting boot?

Make up your mind that for once in your life you will have a boot that satisfies you to the smallest detail -- a boot that does not slip at the heel nor pinch at the toe, a boot that will not wrinkle or run over at the side. Make up your mind that this time you will have a boot that follows perfectly the lines of your foot, that from the very day you first put it on, feels cool and comfortable, and that will retain its trim and stylish appearance under the test of wear.

Dickson boots combine the three features that you have been looking for so long -- style, comfort and wearing quality. They observe so closely the little points that give ease and comfort, that no matter how particular you may be, there is a boot somewhere in our stock that is literally built for your foot. And you will be surprised to find how long it will last. For Dickson boots, whether of patent, gun metal or tan, are made of the very best stock that leather science can produce.

The catalogue you requested is going to you today under separate cover. I want particularly to call your attention to the new "Easy Last" style on page 37. This may be just what you were looking for. But it is only one of the 54 attractive styles you will find illustrated.

Select the style and finish that you like best, then simply fill in on the order form the number, size and width you want, and post to us today. If there are any little peculiarities about your foot, tell us about them. With this information to guide us we will send you, all charges prepaid, the very day that your order is received, a pair of boots that will fit you perfectly.

Do not miss this opportunity to obtain real, genuine boot comfort. Send your order at once -- today.

Yours very truly,

</td></tr>
</table>

troubles and "your" needs, and offers the boot it exploits as an article that will bring "you" satisfaction.

Mrs. Jones puts you off ; Mrs. Smith tells you to wait ; and so it goes—season after season.   You could almost start a new shop with the money lost by local retailers through bad debts.

" Now suppose we could tell you how to stop this ; suppose we could tell you of a simple collection scheme used by one retailer in Birmingham that enabled him to make thirty of his hardest and slowest customers pay up— penny for penny—the many pounds they owed him. Wouldn't you jump at the chance to get it ?

" Now, then, in the book described by the circular enclosed, you can get this very collection system ; the simplest, most successful collection system ever devised—a system that does not require the assistance of an expensive collector ; a system that you yourself can operate, and the only expense is two or three penny stamps "

That is the kind of letter that pulls money from my cash drawer. The guns of attractive argument and effective salesmanship are levelled directly at me. I must either get out of the way or stand and take the shot. I buy because " you and your collections " has been the attitude of the letter. If this concern had pointed their shot somewhere up in the air of foreign interests, there would have been no reason why I should budge an inch, and I wouldn't.

I AM not interested in your affairs until you have shown some interest in mine.   And you can never make me believe that you are really interested in me by everlastingly harping on *we.*

A tire manufacturer answers my inquiry with this : *" We have your favour of the fourteenth stating that you are interested in our advertisement of Wonder tires.*

We are enclosing our Wonder booklet which illustrates and describes our Wonder tread. We would be very glad to give you any further information and our best price. Trusting that you will insist on Wonder tires, we are, yours very truly."

Now I *was* interested in the advertisement, but is there one single reason in that " we " spotted letter why I should continue to be interested, why I should "insist" on having Wonder tires ? What I wanted from that manufacturer was tire talk that applied to *me*. *His* interest in the deal was obvious. It was *mine* that was essential to a sale. And that letter killed what little I had.

Contrast it with this from a manufacturer who would sell me an engine : " *You know what a nuisance it is to set out to equip a boat and find that you haven't got this and you haven't got that. Before you finish, it has cost a quarter or a third more than you estimated.*

"*Customers have often asked us : 'What does your equipment include ? Why don't you make it complete ? ' That's just what we're going to do in future—we are going to ' put in everything.' And what's more, we're going to pay the carriage.*"

That man is talking to *me*. He knows my boat troubles. He's talking to me in my own boat-house, and I read on through his description and sales-argument with an interest approaching fascination, because I feel from the first word that the writer of that letter understands my needs.

—————

TO BE a successful writer you must talk about your customer and his affairs. See that you get the word " you " in the opening sentence of your next letter. For example :

" *You can make a larger profit if you sell Duff's Sugar than if you don't. Your customers want Duff's Sugar and they are going to get it somewhere. You can make big profits by early application* " and so on.

The grocer is interested in this because it offers to put money in his cash-drawer. There is no more interesting proposition to him than that. When he reads this letter he must decide whether he will order and make good profits, or stand idly by while the other fellow gathers in the benefits.

And when you have injected some of the " you " element into your letters, cultivate the ability to get over on the buyer's side and look at your proposition through his eyes. A good salesman never mentions the selling point—he emphasizes the buying point.

You may think it selfish, but I repeat that the nearest subject to me is *me*. The nap hand theme with you is *you*. It is a human trait—as infallible as a physical law.

Personal Good Will

THE machine-finished sale is passing. Buyers prefer to deal man to man. The successful dealer of the future must approach his sales, his letter - writing problems, from the customer's side.

It is not enough to collect to-day's profits, for your competitor is collecting to-morrow's good will.

Part IV

COLLECTION, COMPLAINT, AND ROUTINE LETTERS

Sell Satisfaction

SUCCESS in selling doesn't simply mean goods sold. It means customers satisfied.

It means bills paid outside of court, and complaints handled on square-deal principles. It means treating a man *after* the sale as well as you do before.

Irritating back-talk and aggravating threats never got a good-will settlement nor brought back a disappointed customer; a " slap-on-the-shoulder " attitude drives trade away.

But courtesy, tact, open-minded fairness—disarm antagonism, melt opposition, bring back business.

Be fair. Aim to sell *satisfaction*, and your goods will sell themselves.

CHAPTER XV

Collecting Accounts by Letter

IT is one thing to induce a man to take something that he wants ; it is quite another to induce him to give up something that he wants. Therein lies the vital difference between the sales and the collection letter.

The sales-letter writer has the pleasant task of presenting an article in such an alluring way that the reader is willing to part with his money to own it. The writer of the collection letter, on the other hand, must persuade a man to give up his money for an article which he already has in his possession and from which he has already, in part at least, derived his profit.

He who would do this must bring into play a wide knowledge of human nature that will enable him to use the wise argument in the right place. The common division of debtors into three classes—good, slow, and bad payers—is true enough so far as it goes, but the problem is not so simple as that. Between the two extremes of good and bad paying debtors, there are a thousand gradations, representing men of many different characteristics and circumstances. Each presents an individual problem.

Recognising this, collection managers are coming more and more to see the element of danger in a too strict adherence to the use of form letters. In the handling of a great many small accounts, as in a mail order house or one selling to the consumer on the instalment plan, they are of course an economic necessity ; and in a commercial business also they will always be used in cases where there are no special conditions to be met. But if any account is not fully covered by the regular forms, the wise collection manager will not hesitate to discard the forms, and give personal attention to the account.

———

WHATEVER kind of letter is used—the form or the individual letter—the writer's first care is to give the right tone, dignified and firm, yet considerate and friendly. Getting this right tone into the letter is largely a matter of getting the right perspective on what your customer's relations and his obligation to you really are.

It is a mistake to look upon a just debt as anything but the strictest business obligation. The customer has bought the goods on certain terms and has agreed to pay according to these terms. Especially bad is the practice of asking for payment on the ground that your firm is hard up. The moment you write to a man in this way you thereby put yourself in the same class with your debtor, and you suggest to him a new excuse that he may not have used before. Rather put it this way :

"*Prompt payment of bills by our customers makes it possible for us to sell our goods more cheaply. When our money comes in regularly on the date due, we don't have to make an allowance for extra interest charges and add a percentage to all selling prices to cover the amount. You benefit by the low prices."*

But while it is necessary that you regard the debt as a strict business obligation, it is equally important that you consider the debtor first of all as a customer. A customer's trade is valuable to you until he has shown by a persistent ignoring of your requests for settlement that he cannot or does not intend to pay his bills voluntarily. Under those circumstances his business is not desirable to you in the future, and you are perfectly justified in making a sterner demand for settlement.

Keeping the customer's goodwill is a matter of selecting the proper arguments and using the right tone. It does not mean a week-kneed collection policy or an apologetic attitude. It means making him see the fairness of your position and your readiness to give due consideration to his difficulties. The collection-letter offers many opportunities for the use of little personal touches that give it the tone of friendly interest in the debtor's affairs. If you can make your letter convey the idea that you are interested in him and his welfare, as well as your own, you can insist upon payment without causing resentment. It is these intimate touches that conciliate a man when mere formalities antagonise him.

Now let us remember that not all of these elements appear in every letter; but they represent proved methods of handling a number of situations with which the collection writer is constantly confronted. The completed letter will consist of a combination of these elements that will best meet the requirements of any given case.

Mr. Albert G. Green,

       Manchester

Dear Sir:

     You have been so busy making your pre-
parations for the holiday trade, that you have
doubtless overlooked the fact that your account
with us is somewhat overdue. You have settled
your bills promptly in the past and we feel confident that this reminder will meet with an
equally prompt remittance in this instance.

     How is the Venetian Toilet Soap selling?
Many of our customers are finding this one of the
best money-makers they have handled, not only because of its real merit, but because of the exten-
sive advertising campaign which the manufacturers
are carrying on.

     As you know, we can give you an unusually
good profit on this soap and it should pay you
well to push it during the holiday season. If
you can use another gross of boxes we can ship
them on the day ordered.

     With best wishes for a good season,

        . Very truly yours,

          Spear, Hammond & Co.

An example of a good first collection letter written by the correspondent of a commercial house to a customer who has fallen behind. Note how the selling talk introduced gives the letter a cordial, courteous tone that impresses the customer with his obligation and at the same time lays a basis for more business.

ONE important thing is the notification of the standing of the account. This element appears in practically every collection letter, and usually forms the opening sentence or paragraph. It may be a very informal reminder, conveying the idea that failure to pay is due to a mere oversight, as for instance the letter reproduced on the next page.

Starting with this very conciliatory reminder, the

notification is made more and more emphatic with each succeeding letter of the collection series.

The following is from the second letter of a series :

"*The cheque you were to send me for £18. 5s.—due on your bill of March 12th, has not arrived. No doubt you have overlooked the bill, or have it pigeon-holed for early settlement.*"

In this letter an oversight is again suggested, but such a suggestion is usually far-fetched after the first letter has been unanswered.

This opening from a later letter is still more emphatic :

"*I have sent you frequent statements and letters about the £18. 5s. on your account, which is now two months past due. Yet you have not paid the account or even answered my letters.*"

After this introductory sentence or paragraph containing the notification of how the account stands, the letter proceeds with the collection talk proper. This will vary with the different classes of debtors and with the position of the letter in the series. Naturally, you would not write the same to the good-paying and the bad-paying customer, and the arguments that are suitable for the second letter would not be the ones to use in the fourth.

———

WHEN no response is received from an urgent letter requesting payment by return, a creditor is justified in taking any steps that may seem necessary to force payment. The next letter to the customer should be little more than a notification of this. There is no need to explain why you are placing the account in the hands of a solicitor ; that should be evident on the face of it. Write a note short and imperative :

" We have made (three) requests for payment of the enclosed account. Each one you have ignored. The account is long past due, and yet you have not even given us a reason why you have delayed payment.

" We cannot carry this any longer, and unless it is paid by .... we shall, without further notice, turn it over to our solicitors for collection."

Sometimes you have reason to believe that the debtor may have some valid reason which prevents immediate payment. He may be dissatisfied with the goods or with the treatment his order received, but has not sent in any complaint. Or he may be in temporary difficulty owing to sickness, to unexpected and unforeseeable local conditions which make his own collections slow, etc. If the customer is dissatisfied, the writer invites him to make his complaint known, and also seizes upon this opportunity to impress upon him the firm's desire always to give complete satisfaction to every customer. In the second case, the collection writer asks for a frank explanation, and declares the firm's willingness to make any reasonable arrangements to help him.

Here is the way one correspondent handled a situation of this kind :

" If there are any valid reasons why you are unable to meet this obligation at the present time, let us know at once what they are. When we know just where you stand, some settlement satisfactory to us both can be made."

When such inquiries are sent to the customer, your next procedure will depend upon the nature of his response. If he answers with some just complaint, and that is adjusted, the chances are that he will settle the

bill and thus close the transaction. If he writes that
he has met with temporary reverses that he could not
have foreseen, the next step is to suggest some way out
of the difficulty, such as to take his note with interest ;
to ask for part payment or payment in regular instalments ; or to offer to take back the goods and cancel
the bill. A typical paragraph offering one of these
suggestions follows :

" *Since you are unable to pay the whole of your bill now,
we will let you settle for the rest with your personal accept-
ances, bearing interest at 6%. Send us the £75 which you
can pay now. For the remainder, £150, you can send us
at the same time one bill payable in sixty days ; or two
bills equal in amount, payable respectively ; or three
equal in amount, payable respectively in thirty, sixty, and
ninety days. Choose the plan which suits you best. This
arrangement will help you over your present difficulty.*"

AN appeal that will reach many debtors is one that
suggests the bad effect of non-payment on their business, or, conversely, the good effect of prompt payment.
In other words, it makes the man think of his own loss
or gain. In this case, the suggestion of loss is usually
more emphatic than that of gain. His guilty conscience
—unless it is hardened by long misuse—will reinforce
the appeal. The loss that is suggested may be refusal
of future credit by our firm, the damage to his credit
with other houses, the loss of financial standing in his
community, and similar matters of vital importance to
a business man. One firm writes :

" *You want to keep your credit perfectly clear. The
only sure way to do this, as you know, is to pay your bills
promptly as they fall due. Any delay is liable to cause*"

a bad impression, which you will find very difficult to get rid of later on."

Another firm uses this :

" We desire to effect a settlement of this account in an easy and amicable way. Giving publicity to it would not help us, but it would certainly bring discredit to you among your friends and neighbours."

This last letter contains not only an appeal to his loss in his business relations, but also one to his personal pride.

Then, again, the suggestion may be made that by paying he can save himself annoyance and trouble. This may be the annoyance of getting more " dunning " letters, or the trouble and expense of a lawsuit.

In the final letter of a series, this suggestion becomes a definite statement that legal proceedings will be promptly begun, as :

" This is our final notice, and should we fail to hear from you within ten days, the matter will be placed with our solicitor with instructions to take any steps necessary to effect a quick settlement."

A NOTHER element of the collection letter is that which urges the debtor " to do it now," to pay up at once. Some writers content themselves with an urgent request for prompt payment ; as, " Please give this matter your immediate attention " ; or " Send us your cheque or postal order to-day." Others go further and suggest some means for making the act of paying easy ; for example, " Don't bother to write a letter. Just pin your cheque to this note and post it to me."

The " easy-to-pay " methods have the advantage of

minimising the actual physical effort needed to make the payment. They are effective because they forestall man's inclination to put off a task unless it is made very easy to do. In this respect the collection writer has taken over one of the devices of the advertisement and sales-letter writers, who have long recognised that the return coupon and the return post card are among their most valuable aids in getting returns.

———

COLLECTION letters on instalment accounts differ from commercial letters chiefly in that the purchase is a single transaction and there is frequently little probability of future business. For this reason the sales element is largely lacking. Reason for settlement must run on two points—the buyer's honour and his obligation to abide by his contract.

The prime aim is to prevent the debtor from getting behind in more than one instalment. When two remain unpaid, the amount is doubly difficult to collect, and if three accumulate, some summary action or " cash up " offer is almost absolutely necessary to make the account profitable.

Because instalment propositions are usually sold to all buyers on a uniform basis or payment, form-letters may be used far more extensively than in commercial work. In fact, debtors and their degrees of indebtedness may be so classified that a series may be prepared which will meet almost any objection and apply to nearly every situation.

One collection man has divided his accounts into three classes—those on which only one payment has been made, those on which more than half have been made, and those on which only a very small amount is still outstanding. For each class he has prepared a series of five letters and they have been so carefully developed through experience with instalment buyers that they are in a vast majority of instances as well suited as a personally dictated letter.

It is customary among houses doing an instalment business on a monthly basis not to begin a strictly collection series until a copy of the monthly statement marked " Second Notice " has failed to bring a response. If fifteen days pass after this second notice without a reply, the first letter should be sent calling the debtor's attention to the fact that the amount has probably been overlooked and requesting immediate attention. It is not a bad plan to point out in this letter in a courteous way the importance of keeping these instalments paid up promptly.   One house follows its request with a paragraph something like this :

" *Perhaps you have overlooked the fact that in signing this contract you agreed to send us a remittance regularly each month without fail, until your account has been paid in full.   This, however, was the agreement, and we have naturally planned on receiving the payments in this manner.*

" *We feel certain that for your own convenience you will find it more satisfactory to adhere to this plan, for if you allow two or more instalments to accrue, and are compelled to send us the whole amount in one remittance, it may prove inconvenient.   We shall appreciate it if you will settle the overdue payment at once, and see that future instalments reach us promptly each month as they fall due.*"

If a courteous letter like this does not bring at least a reply as to why the payment has not been made within ten or fifteen days, a second letter considerably more urgent in tone should be sent.

Beyond this stage, your procedure should be guided by the surrounding circumstances. Before proceeding to an attempt to force collection many firms use what is called a "Cash-up" inducement, that is, a discount or an article free for an immediate settlement.

"*I am going to make one more effort,*" writes one collector for a publishing house, "*to reach an amicable agreement with you. If you will send me at once a cheque covering the balance due on your account with us, I will send you at absolutely no expense to you and as evidence of my appreciation of your fulfilling your part of the contract without unpleasantness, a copy of Wood's ' Commercial Law,' a volume which every business man should have on his desk. Only an exceptional combination of circumstances enables me to do this, and we have only a few copies of the book available. If you wish to take advantage of this offer, you should let me hear from you at once. Simply enclose your cheque with this letter and post to-day.*"

If your delinquent accepts this offer, well and good. If he does not, your only open road is to go to court. But usually it is wise to make one more effort to touch the debtor's sense of respect. Remember always that most men want to pay their debts, and do not consider any man dishonest until he has proved himself so. The debtor who has been harried and aggravated by the ordinary "give-me-my-money" letter will have a pleasant surprise if you show him a personal understanding of his case. And your cordial willingness to be reasonable will get your money while the man who flies to early threats waits for his.

Then when the time comes to threaten legal action, do so bluntly and positively. Give the debtor a definite number of days in which to pay, then turn the account over to your solicitor or a collection agency.

CHAPTER XVI

How to Answer Complaints

IF your customers are worth having, they are worth satisfying, and if your goods are worth selling, it is worth your while to demonstrate that fact to your customers, even after they have bought your offerings and you have their money. No legitimate business transaction is really completed until the customer is satisfied with his purchase. A satisfied old customer often represents more potential business than a bookful of untried prospects. If you have given him a square deal, he never stops saying good things about your business ; but if you have left him dissatisfied, he never stops driving it away.

And it is not such a hard matter to show a man that you have given him at least all you have agreed to give him, if you go about it in a courteous, tactful way. Most people have more than a spark of reasonableness in them and an ability to recognise a fair proposition when they see it. If they haven't, they haven't the possibilities of being good customers, and no concession, however generous, would ever satisfy them.

Good answers to complaints, like good collection letters, are largely a matter of attitude. There is no use assuming a high and mighty position and trying to make all your customers conform to your ideas of what a square deal is. It is better to assume a fair but open-minded position and then show each complainant that he really sees things as you do after all.

Nor is there anything to be gained by allowing yourself to become aroused over anything that a man with a grumble may write you. For back talk simply aggravates the customer instead of pacifying him and leaves the grievance farther from settlement than it was before. And what is more you ought not to give the unreasonable grumbler the satisfaction of knowing that he has stirred your temper.

———

ONE thing, do not be too suspicious of every complaint that comes over your desk. Remember that when your customer wrote his letter, he believed he had cause for doing so, and that the chances are he did have. Remember that *most* people want to be square with you, that *most* people are honest, and that by far the greater share of the complaints you get have a real cause at bottom. The fault may not be yours, but that is no reason why you should snap up a man for telling you about it. If you are not to blame, the proper thing to do is to find out where the trouble lies, and help the customer to straighten out the difficulty.

And even though a man seems to have no cause for complaint, be just as good-natured about showing him where he is wrong as you would if he had a real grievance against you. Everyone else feels about the same as you do when you get a complaint that appears unjust and unwarranted. Your first impatience prompts you to say to yourself, "Oh, I'll show this fellow. I'll let him know that he can't talk that way to me. I'll write him a letter that he won't forget in a hurry."

And suppose you do. He gets the letter, reads it, lays you out to everyone within hearing distance and sends back your goods. And the remotest chance of ever making a good customer out of him is gone.

But suppose you say to yourself when you get a letter like that : "Now, if this man knew as much about business as I do he wouldn't make a complaint like this. He writes this way either because he's ignorant of propriety and business courtesy or because he doesn't realise that mistakes will happen in the best regulated businesses. So I'll write him a letter that will wake him up, maybe, to what a business transaction really is. And I'll do it by giving him an example of cordial business courtesy." Then carry out just that idea, and you'll not only feel better about it yourself, but the chances are your attitude will bring back a customer who was ready to slip away at the slightest provocation.

ALL genuine complaints can pretty nearly be traced to two sources : real grievances and misunderstandings, the latter often due to ignorance of business methods or requirements. In either case it is to your interest to settle the complaint satisfactorily and retain the good will of the customer.

And to do this there are certain points that you must invariably consider. In the first place, answer promptly. An immediate reply goes a long way toward impressing a man with your sincere desire to see him satisfied. If he isn't specific enough in his complaint to enable you to answer fully, write at once for further information.

If it is going to take you several days to investigate, write him first and tell him what you are doing. Every day that a complaint hangs over it becomes increasingly hard to handle, while quick attention will preclude many possibilities of future unpleasantness and will be appreciated by the customer.

Second, take the complaint seriously. For instance, if a man orders twenty reams of paper from you and on receipt of it writes that it is not like the sample he ordered from, don't say : *" Dear Sir : Your eyesight must be defective. The paper you ordered is certainly identically the same stock as the sample you named. Take it to the window and look again."*

If you do that you not only insult his intelligence, but you may be getting yourself in a bad position, for there's just a chance that a mistake was made in the stock or shipping room and that the customer is right.

Better write him something like this :

" Dear Sir : We are surprised to learn that the Golden bond does not seem to match exactly the sample from which you ordered. Could you by any chance have got this confused with Gordon bond which is next to it in the sample book ? These two lines are very similar in finish and the fact that there is also a similarity in the names has given rise to errors of this kind once or twice before. I wish you would refer to the book and see whether this might be the cause of the discrepancy.

" If it is not and you will send us a sample of the order you received, we will have the trouble looked up here immediately. We are always very careful to check over outgoing stock and see that it is just what is ordered, but we realise that an error might have been made somewhere in the process of packing and shipping and we will be more than glad to correct it." See the difference ? That

not only protects you but it shows the man your serious interest in putting matters right.

THE next vitally important point is that you take the customer's viewpoint. Look at the trouble through his eyes. Just as in a sales-letter you can win a prospect's confidence by opening with a statement that he recognises as a matter of fact and then from that point gradually leading him to your proposition, so in answering a complaint, you can start out by agreeing with him and gradually lead him around to your way of looking at the question.

If you don't—if you state your position first and try to drag him to it, you are sure to antagonise.

A publisher sold a business book to a clerk in a railway office and the young man on receiving it complained that while the volume might be all right for a man in an established business, it was of no practical value to him.

Now the publisher might have answered that young man after this fashion :

" *Dear Sir : Don't think that because the book seems of no use to you, we are going to take it back and refund your money. You certainly understood the nature of this book before you ordered it and if you didn't want it, that was the time to say so instead of now after we have gone to the expense of sending it to you and after the deal is closed. Under the circumstances, we cannot take the book back* "

Understand, that's what he *might* have said, because that's just the tone in which many a complaint is answered every day. But he actually wrote the young man in this manner :

" Dear Sir :

" I believe I understand perfectly just how you feel about the book.   You feel that because your position is a detail one, because your work is limited in its scope, the book is too comprehensive to help you very much just now.   And that would seem, at first thought, a very just objection.   But in reality, because your work is limited now, and because the book is comprehensive, aren't you that very man the book will help most ?

" Every man wants to get out of the rut, to grow, to develop into something better.   Yet who is the man who wins promotion ?   Is it the clerk whose work is limited to his own routine of details ?   No, it is the man who knows not only his own work, but that of the man above him. And that is just what this book will enable you to learn. For it gives you the experiences of the most successful men in the country, it describes in detail their methods and the results."

And so it ran on, showing the customer exactly how he could put the book to profitable use.

NOW in reply to either of those letters the young man would have kept the book ; but in the first instance he would have kept it because he had to, in the second he did keep it because he *wanted* to.   And that is the difference between a poor complaint letter and a good one.

" Messrs. Bordens, Ltd.

Liverpool.

Gentlemen :

The last consignment of Flor de Majesta cigars I received from you have arrived in very poor condition. It is evident that these cigars have been exposed to the damp and as they were ordered on behalf of a special customer, I feel very annoyed about it. This is not the first complaint I have had to make concerning your goods and I am afraid that your house is not taking the care over its stock as formerly. My customer requires the cigars urgently and as matters stand I am in danger of losing him if a consignment of the old quality is not quickly forthcoming. I am returning the last lot by carrier.

Yours faithfully,"

Here is an effective reply :

"*Dear Sir :—We have your letter of the 26th inst. and have since received the cigars complained of.*

"*We really cannot see that you are justified in your allegation that these goods have been exposed to damp. Our precautions against such a possibility are made with too much care and method to admit an occurrence of the kind, and we can only conclude that your customer is one of those individuals who must have his occasional grumble.*

"*Complaints against the quality of our goods are very rare indeed and when investigated are usually discovered to be either altogether unfounded, or of the most trivial description.*

"*Nevertheless, although we cannot honestly admit the justice of your claim, we are forwarding another consignment of Flor de Majesta and trust these will give satisfaction.*

"*Trusting that they will arrive without delay and promising you that this will not happen again, we are,*

Yours faithfully,"

These three letters are excellent examples of how trade may be lost through untactful handling of a complaint and how it may be saved when skill and care are used. The first letter was sent by a retail tobacconist to his wholesale house.   It was to his mind at least a just complaint.   But observe how a correspondent at the house answered it.

"*Dear Sir :—A complaint about the condition of our Flor de Majesta cigars comes to us as a distinct shock. Coming as it does from an old and valued customer makes it the still less agreeable.*

"*We realise that your customer would not smoke Flor de Majestas unless he were a keen judge of what constitutes a good cigar.   It may be then that for once our elaborate precautions against possibilities of exposure to damp have broken down, although how they can have done so, we are at a loss to understand.*

"*What we are chiefly concerned with is to make matters right with the greatest possible speed.   On receipt of your letter we forwarded by rail a consignment of cigars which we feel sure your customer will enjoy as he has enjoyed the previous lots.*

"*We assure you that our care of stock is just as keen as it ever was, to say the least, and we shall be anxious to prove this to you by the exercise of extra vigilance in the execution of your future orders.*

Yours faithfully"

A NOTHER vitally important point—do not argue with anybody.   If the customer is in the wrong, show him courteously where he is wrong, but *explain*, do not argue.   If a customer writes you that goods he ordered of you to be sent two weeks before, have not been received and that he doubts whether you ever sent them, don't reply by saying :

"*If the goods you ordered have not reached you, it is certainly due to no fault of ours.   We sent them promptly and hold the Railway Co.'s receipt to prove it. You should know that goods are often lost by the railway companies even though the greatest care is shown in preparing them for transit. Under the circumstances, we think you are hardly warranted in accusing us of not having sent them. When we say a thing you may depend upon it.*

" However, inasmuch as you say you did not get the goods, we are duplicating the order and would ask you to notify us if the first order turns up."

This letter, which is typical of many that go through the post every day, illustrates not only the bad policy of arguing with your man, but also the mistake of first antagonising him, and then in the end granting what he asks.

If you are going to concede the justice of his complaint at all or if you are going to grant him his claim simply as a favour, do it cheerfully and make the customer realise that you *are* giving him more than what is justly due to him.

Write to this man whose goods have not reached him, something in this style :

" Dear Sir : You are certainly justified in complaining of not having received the goods you ordered fully two weeks ago. You have been very considerate in waiting so long, and we appreciate fully how you feel about the matter now.

" It seems to us that there can be no question that the fault lies with the Railway Co. The receipt we hold shows that the goods were received by them in good condition the very day your order reached us. We knew you were in urgent need of this stock and we made a special request for quick service in selecting and packing it.

" As your experience has probably shown you, many concerns hold that their responsibility ceases the moment

the goods are despatched to the Railway Co. However, we always consider the interests of our customers as more important than a technical privilege of this kind and we never consider a transaction closed until the goods are received and found to be entirely satisfactory.

" So we are having a duplicate shipment packed and forwarded to you to-day. We are confident that these goods will reach you almost as soon as this letter, and in perfect condition.

" The matter of delay in the previous shipment we shall take up with the Railway Co. at once and shall ask them to trace the goods. In the meantime, should they chance to reach you we will thank you to return them to us, charges forward."

There you have an answer that not only satisfies the customer in every point, but it is bound to make him realise that you are more than fair, and the incidental talk about your service gives the letter a little sales-value that the customer isn't likely to forget.

———

POSSIBLY the best way to get the right attitude in answering a complaint is to stop and consider how you would handle the customer if he came personally into your office. Certainly you wouldn't pick a quarrel with him, you wouldn't let yourself be other than courteous and polite throughout his call. And you would take him all through the house if necessary just to demonstrate how sincerely desirous the firm was of giving him a square deal.

Remember that the next time you answer a complaint. Picture the customer beside your desk. Then *talk* to him. You'll find your old time itch to be vindictive gradually disappearing and the results vastly more satisfactory to you and the customer alike.

CHAPTER XVII

Routine Letters and the "Paragraph System"

SALES, collection, and complaint letters—these make up by far the most important parts of a business's correspondence. But there are scores of letters issuing from an office every day which are not any of these ; they are rather "routine" letters, arising out of the commonplace details of doing business intimately connected with the actual conduct of affairs. Letters of general trading, developing into contracts between merchant, manufacturer, and customer ; market quotations, replies to inquiries, requests for information, purchasing letters, and acknowledgments.

Letters regarding inquiries are so varied that they cannot fit into definite rules. The reply should answer each part of the inquiry separately. It is not sufficient to send a price list and tell the inquirer to find what he wants ; the reply should direct attention to the specific information and be written, moreover, on the principles of all good sales letters.   ·

The letter ordering goods usually has three elements : the list of goods, instructions for forwarding, the intimation of mode of payment. The details of goods should be precise in quantity, style, size, price, and identifying number, if any, being set forth, and with each item in a separate line. A long list can be put on a separate sheet.

A letter should state how delivery is to be made—by parcel post, carrier, or rail. The route is sometimes specified, and the expected date of delivery. When cash is enclosed with the order, the fact should be mentioned.

————

PURCHASING letters, ordering factory materials or goods for stock, fall into general classes. Some letters ask for quotations, stating what is wanted, and often enclosing a sample. Here is an example calculated to gain attention :

" *We expect to be in the market shortly for* 150,000 *statements printed exactly like the enclosed sample. Knowing that you have special facilities for producing this kind of work, we believe you can give us a satisfactory price on the job and therefore ask you to submit a quotation at your earliest convenience. We shall supply the paper.*"

The actual order for goods required for stock or factory is often on a printed form and an accompanying letter is only needed when any departure from the usual routine is involved. Such letters often abound in technicalities. For instance :—

" *Please furnish us, subject to the following prices, specifications, and conditions, your best quality open-hearth steel boiler rivets, all button head :*

$$6 \; cwt. \; \tfrac{7}{8}'' \quad 2\tfrac{1}{2}''$$
$$4 \; cwt. \; \tfrac{7}{8}'' \quad 2\tfrac{3}{4}''$$

" *This material is to be invoiced at* 1¼d. *per lb. net f.o.r. your mill, carriage allowed to Rugby, terms* 30-2-10 *as in your quotation No. 8643, of August 20. We note you can deliver two days after receipt of order and count on you to dispatch these rivets not later than Thursday of this week."*

Besides the quotation and order letter an adjustment letter may be needed. This letter may give notice of some mistake in filling the order, such as the substitution of inferior quality, or an error in quantity or price, and it suggests some method of adjustment.

Purchasing letters, which are in reality contracts, may be more formal and less personal than letters which seek to persuade or satisfy a customer. Brevity and clearness distinguish them.

A VERY common routine letter is that acknowledging an order. This tells the customer that the order has been received and completes the contract in a legal sense. A courteous expression of thanks should be incorporated. If the order cannot be filled entirely, reasons and explanations are given. If the goods are not sent as ordered, the statement will do two things :

First, it will give you the reason for not carrying out the order. The reason may be that the line has been discontinued ; the goods are temporarily out of stock ; not enough money was enclosed ; or the order is held up until the cash or further credit information is received. In case cash is required before shipment, care must be taken to base your request on strict business consideration.

Secondly, the letter will tell or suggest how the difficulty is to be adjusted. The customer may be notified that the money is being returned, and a revised catalogue sent to prevent future order of discontinued lines ; or he may be requested to send more money, pay cash, or give credit references, as the case demands.

The letter frequently closes with a few words inviting further orders. The purpose of this part of the letter is to give a touch of personal interest to the acknowledgment. Sometimes, however, this personal close is omitted.

———————

LIKE barometers, our letters and also our speech take at least a part of the tone and tenor of our inside feelings.

When we feel right, we write right. We put into our letters the cheery optimism we hold in our mind. We are courteous, considerate, tactful, suave.

If a customer asks of us an unreasonable concession, we do not tell him so point-blank ; we put the pellet of fact in the sugar of tact. We inform him " No ! " but we inform him pleasantly, slighting none of the little kid-glove courtesies that give a warm, velvet, cordial touch, even to the letter of rejection.

But we do not always feel right. When we are tired and discouraged, when things have not gone entirely to our liking ; when aggravation after aggravation has pricked our mind and goaded our temper to the end of endurance, it is hard indeed to still use the kid-glove customs, the gentle word, the kindly manner, the cordial style. We are sour inside, we have the " vinegar brain." How can we still write in the treacle vain ?

That is why it is an extremely difficult problem to set a certain high standard for our correspondence, and to keep every letter keyed up to this standard. And in a house where there are numbers of correspondents, each of different temperament, all perhaps feeling a shade different, is it any wonder that we seldom find a large concern whose correspondence is evenly good, day in and day out ?

Now, then, suppose we had always on tap, for use in fair weather and foul, in good times and in bad, the best things that have ever been written or said about the affairs of our business, the best paragraphs on our policy, our terms, our credit, our methods, our integrity, our goods, each and every paragraph a masterpiece, written when we were in the very acme of good nature.

Could you put down in three figures or four a sum that would adequately represent the value of such a system to you ?

———

IN every business house there are a certain number of business questions that are asked over and over again, a number of times a day. There are certain classes of inquiries that require the same kind of handling ; there are certain classes of slow-paying customers who have to be written to in about the same vein. There are a hundred letters we send out each day that could all start just alike, and many of them give the same information throughout. Compare your letters and note how nearly identical they run. Why take separate time for each ? Why not choose the best ? If we had a complete set of paragraphs to answer every business question asked us in our post, it would be an easy matter to pick out the different paragraphs needed to convey to each correspondent the desired information, then fit them together, judiciously and discriminately, into a perfect letter.

The great trouble with most " paragraph letters," however, is that they seem machine-made instead of human-dictated. When the author of them sat down to put into permanent form the thoughts of every-day dictation, he lost his natural, easy, personal tone, and straightway became formal. But this can be overcome by the method of formation as described in a succeeding paragraph.

Our first step in compiling our paragraph book should be to determine exactly what paragraphs are needed. No man can do this by running over in his mind the kinds of questions that are asked him frequently, because the fact of the matter is, no man really realises how much material he does constantly dictate over and over again. When the writer started to put in his paragraph system, he was sceptical as to whether it was really worth while to bother with it. He thought that most of his letters were " unusual letters," and required special dictation. But when he finally dissected and analysed his correspondence, he found that there was scarcely a single question or point brought up in any letter that had not been brought up a number of times before. And to-day, with the exception of his personal and important letters, his entire correspondence, averaging seventy-five letters a day, is answered wholly with form paragraphs.

THE way to find out what paragraphs are needed is to have an extra carbon copy made of every letter answered for about two weeks. That should give you at least one sample of nearly every sort of letter received in the general run of correspondence.

It is well to set aside a goodly half-day to go through these carbon copies. First classify them as to their general character, putting all inquiry letters together, all complaint letters together, all general letters, etc.

Now further classify under "Sales Correspondence," "Wants to Know Price," "Asks About Terms," "Do We Prepay Carriage," "Do We Take Back Unsatisfactory Goods," etc. Now cut up your letters into paragraphs, and put all paragraphs of one kind into one pile.

By looking through these piles of paragraphs, it will be easy to see what paragraphs are dictated often enough to deserve a regular form paragraph. When you have got together a complete list of the form paragraphs needed, you can then pick out from the paragraphs in the piles the best one to answer each given question, polish it up, and bring it up to the "masterpiece" standard. When your paragraphs are completed they are put into a book and numbered, so that, in specifying the paragraphs needed to answer a letter, you simply give your typist the numbers of them.

Secure a large scrap-book with heavy manila pages, and wide, blank indexes. Or, better still, get a book with no indexes and cut the indexes for yourself with a pen-knife. Place on the first page—page one—the word "Starts, "and write this plainly on the thumb index.

This page should contain all the good "beginnings" you have ever composed for starting off a letter, from the commonest "Replying to yours of the tenth" to the most elaborate and original introductions.

Paste these paragraphs down on the first page, numbering them 1-1, 1-2, 1-3, the first figure denoting the page and the second the number of the paragraph.

Take the second page and label it with the name of another class of paragraphs such as "Generalities," pasting all paragraphs on general facts about your goods.

Now go through the remainder of the book, labeling

each page with the name of a class of paragraphs, such as " Terms," " Prices," " Don't like quality," " Complaints on conditions," " Wants special concessions," " Is buying of competitor," " Buys cheaper elsewhere," and all the other classifications suggested by your work.

As you paste a paragraph on a given page, be sure to number it both according to its place on the page and the number of the page itself. The third paragraph on page 8, for example, should be numbered 8–3. Thus, when you name this paragraph to your typist, she can turn to the paragraph at once.

THE results, both in quantity and quality of work, that a good paragraph system will accomplish in a correspondence department are almost beyond belief. With its use even the dullest correspondent can be made to produce letters that rank in brilliance and tone with those of the best-paid advertising writer. Moreover, there is no varying of your correspondence with your moods. You can growl out the numbers of the paragraphs or laugh them out, but the customers will still get the same paragraphs. You may feel dull or bright, sluggish or alert, it matters not to your correspondence, for you answer it with paragraphs that are always the same, always your best, always your strongest argument, or the smoothest diplomacy that could be composed through hours of previous thought and study.

From the standpoint of time- and labour-saving features it does not need much explanation to show that the paragraph system will provide innumerable advantages for both correspondent and typist. One man with the paragraph system and three typists has been known to handle more work than three men and four typists without "the automatic correspondent " to aid them.

CHAPTER XVIII

Developing a Follow-up Series

" IF the fish don't bite, keep changing the bait. If they don't bite then, change your fishing-hole." This is sound advice for every amateur fisherman, as any grey-haired angler will tell you. It is equally sound philosophy for selling by mail, as every successful salesman knows.

The object of your selling campaign may be to make a certain class of prospects buy your goods through a series of letters directed at that one class. Or the object may be to pull orders from many classes of prospects in the same list by means of a series of letters each one of which convinces a different class. In both cases the success of the campaign is due essentially to the fact that the salesman approaches his project each time from a different angle. He changes his bait. He presents his proposition from a different point of view. This is the heart of the whole matter. He hopes that one of his arguments will arouse an interest that will result in orders from them. Another argument will get a response from another class, and so on. He recognises that men are not all alike, and that it is a waste of time and money to keep trying to reach them all by the same appeal.

Then if a change of bait doesn't work, he changes his fishing hole.

A single sales-letter cannot be expected to exhaust the selling possibilities of a list. It will get orders or inquiries from people who are already familiar with the article and are easily convinced that they want it. Just how many will respond will depend on the nature of the proposition—upon the kind of article and the special inducement that is offered. If the goods are of universal or general value, and an especially attractive price is made, the percentage should be comparatively large. If the article is new or if it involves the expenditure of considerable money, the customer must be led more or less gradually to see that it is worth the money to him.

F OLLOW-UP letters hammer away, letter after letter, on one article or line of goods. A follow-up is carried on for the purpose of selling a certain article or line of goods to a list of prospects, and it makes continued and varied appeals to them until the sales possibilities are exhausted—until the returns are so small that a continuation of the campaign will not pay.

Each letter in the series should make a new appeal and present a new argument. Each should emphasize one point. Other points—supplementary selling talk— may be added, but these are to be subordinates to the main argument. Also, as the series progresses, the preceding arguments may be re-stated briefly from time to time, but these, too, should not be made prominent enough to distract the attention from the main point to which this letter is devoted.

The arrangement of the arguments in a series of follow-up letters—that is, the order in which the letters are sent out—is an important matter. It has been proved by tests that a change in the order affects the pulling power of the series. The most effective arrangement cannot always be determined *a priori*. The most that you can do when you map out a letter campaign is to arrange the letters tentatively in a certain order, which is based upon the experience gained from previous campaigns, or upon the testimony of salesmen as to the arguments they have found most effective.

However, don't spend your money in posting this series to your full list of prospects until you have tested it on a small list. Send it out to, say, five hundred or a thousand names, the number depending upon the scope of your campaign. Then keep a careful record of the returns from each letter. If the test list has been so selected that it is a representative one, the percentage of returns should be about the same from the large list. Consequently you now know which are the stronger letters and which are the weaker. Then on the basis of this test rearrange your series, and if necessary re-write your less successful letters.

IN this arrangement do not make the mistake of using all your stronger arguments in the earlier letters of the series. The first letter should, of course, be a strong one, for it must not only get orders from as large a percentage of prospects as possible and thus save the expense of a further campaign, but it should also arouse sufficient interest, among the readers who are not yet ready to buy, to insure attention for the succeeding letters. Then reserve one or two of the more effective arguments for the latter part of the series, for otherwise you will close with an anti-climax. Good selling talk will be required to bring into line the prospects who have resisted the appeals of the earlier letters.

The series as now arranged is ready to be sent out to the complete mailing list. Each letter will bring orders from some prospects, inquiries from others, and from still others no reply at all. The first class are transferred from your prospect to your customers' list. The last will be retained to receive the following letters of the series. The second class, those making inquiries, will require a different procedure.

A prospect has indicated interest in some phase of the proposition and perhaps has made inquiries about special points.

To him, a new letter, not included in the original series, will be sent. This will, of course, answer his question fully, and perhaps present new points. The subsequent procedure with this man will depend upon the nature of his question. Perhaps his is a special case which requires individual attention throughout. But if it indicates a field of interest not covered by the original series and broad enough to warrant such a procedure, a new series of letters will be sent to him, which will draw their arguments from the new field of interest.

THE first letter of a series is frequently more comprehensive than the later ones, for it must contain enough information to give the reader a definite idea of the article or proposition. Hence in this one the description of the article or explanation of what it will do is, in many sales series, made full and complete. The later letters usually contain less general description, and will lay emphasis on persuasion—show the reader the benefit he will derive from the article—and on inducement. These are, of course, important in the first letter also ; and, likewise, a fresh statement of an important point or points in the description is not out of place in any letter. Each letter has a two-fold purpose—to make the sale and to pave the way for the following letters.

The length of the letters cannot be set arbitrarily for all cases. Theoretically, the ideal length would be not more than one typewritten page, but many letters of two and even more pages have been effective. In general it may be said that a first letter in a series answering an inquiry may safely be made fairly long. The reader has indicated his interest, and if the correspondent uses ordinary care and skill, he should be able to write a detailed letter without sacrificing that interest. The length varies, too, with the class of readers ; as, for example, a letter to a farmer may usually be made longer than one to a hurried business man. However, if you are in doubt as to the proper length of letters, don't guess—make a test. Then you shall have definite information on which to base your judgment.

WE have spoken of the value of testing a follow-up series, both as to the length of the letters and the pulling powers of the different arguments. How is such an experiment conducted ? Send your series to a list of five hundred or a thousand names, selected from localities which you think represent average business possibilities. In this selection you will be guided by your experience in previous selling campaigns, by the reports of salesmen, and by your general knowledge of business conditions in your field. But remember—don't select the best localities or the poorest ; select the average. If you do this, your returns from the test should represent about the proportion of replies that you will get from your complete mailing list—if conditions are the same.

This matter of conducting the test and the complete campaign under similar conditions is important. The three most essential considerations to keep in mind are general business conditions, local conditions, and the time when the prospect receives the letters. For instance, if the test is made during a period of business prosperity, and in the interim between the test and the mailing to the complete list some event occurs which causes a retrenchment among business men, the results of your test will not agree with those of the larger list. The same will be true if local condition or other cause produces hard times in any locality. Also the number of replies will vary with the time when the letter reaches the prospect. Here again you can test to find out the best day to post your letters.

A test is easy to conduct, and its results are indicative to a high degree of accuracy of the returns later from the complete list. With such a convenient and cheap means of finding out the weak and strong points in your follow-up series, there is no excuse for the reckless expenditure of money on expensive, untried campaigns.

———

BUT the follow-up is not confined to selling goods. Wherever there is a shilling to be spent, or a shilling to be collected, information to be gathered, or a public to be educated—there is a place for the follow-up. The uses of the follow-up are infinite and applicable to nearly all departments and activities of business interest. The follow-up means a recurrent appeal on the same subject to the same person until the object aimed at is attained.

BOOKS ON BUSINESS

Published by A. W. SHAW CO., LTD.

43, Shoe Lane, London, E.C.

TO-DAY you need no longer solve your business problems alone and unaided, by slow and costly accumulation of personal experience. For among the thousands of businesses the world over, most of the problems and obstacles and needs that you face in your business every day have already been faced by other men, and have been successfully solved by means of the right methods and actions.

And you now have the recorded experiences of these successful men to turn to for help and guidance. For the best of these solutions of every-day business problems have been gathered together in a series of business books. In these books the latest and best plans and methods actually used by the keenest men and most successful firms for carrying on every sort of detail of business activity, have been sought out for you and are described in plain practical language and clear illustrations so that you can apply them to your own work and business at once.

This series of books covers practically every kind and activity of business—organisation and management, production and manufacture, selling and advertising, accounting and office methods, buying and financing, credits and collections, wholesaling and retailing, correspondence, administration, efficiency and scientific management.

You may turn to these books and find exactly the little idea you need at the moment—or a complete plan for a new policy. And who knows but what just one small idea or a single big policy from one of these books put into practice in your business may be of greater profit to you than years of experimental effort—may open great markets, lead to profit-making economies and efficiencies, save you a crippling loss or turn failure into success.

BUSINESS men of yesterday had no established methods, no formulated principles, no guiding experience. There was only one course open to them : to go forward and try—painfully and slowly to gather their own individual experience by costly trials and re-trials.

But business is passing out of that slow-moving, often-failing, and many-risks period. Facts about business operations have been gathered and analysed and correlated. The right methods have been discovered—the wrong methods branded. The pitfalls and shoals are being marked out, and the sure ways charted. The systems and plans that have proved good in actual use have been analysed and their basic principles discovered.

To-day you can find those proved plans and known facts, you can learn the experience and successful practice of others, in books.

Look through the list of books on the following pages and see which ones will help you to-day in your business. You can obtain them from your bookseller or direct from the publishers.

A SERIES of intensely practical books, each covering completely one definite subject of business and giving the latest and most usable ideas and methods regarding that branch of business. Every plan and method described is taken out of actual successful experience : the ideas and methods are so clearly and specifically explained that they can at once be applied in your own daily work.

The volumes are of uniform size and binding, 128 to 160 pages each, 5 inches by $7\frac{3}{8}$ inches, printed from readable type on good book paper, bound in full cloth, cover in colours.

Price, 2/6 each net ; postage, 3d. extra.

How to Organise Business

A CLEAR and elementary explanation of organisation principles and operating methods for the whole field of business. Analyses and describes the elements of organisation, division into departments, lines of responsibility and authority. Taking each department individually, it describes in detail the methods and systems used, covering every department of a business and an office. Reproduces the charts, rulings, and forms used in operating each system. Whatever department of your business you want to re-organise, wherever you need a new system, whenever you want to perfect some point of routine—refer to this invaluable book and it will give you the exact system you want.

How to Write Letters that Win

COVERS the whole subject of business correspondence in a practical and common-sense way ; shows how to use letters profitably in every department of business. Explains in detail the elements of a good letter, and step by step how to compose it. Tells vividly, clearly, and concretely by actual examples how to write every type of business letter—sales and advertising, collection and adjustment, routine and general letters. Takes your everyday correspondence and shows you how to answer it most effectively. Reproduces 247 actual letters, model paragraphs, follow-ups, and clever ideas that have won goodwill, sold goods, collected money, and adjusted complaints.

How to Run a Shop at a Profit

THIS is the most helpful book ever published for the shop-keeper. For it tells not merely how to make more money by increasing trade and selling more goods, but also how to organise and manage a shop so as to make a larger and surer profit. It is a practical book, for it is a collection of the best ideas and methods and plans of 62 shrewd and successful retailers—their actual tested and found-successful methods for systematising their shops, replacing guesswork with proved plans and figures, increasing turnover, reducing expenses, and so enlarging their profits. It shows how these 62 men met and solved the same problems that confront every retailer to-day.

How to Write Advertisements

ANALYSES effective advertisement writing and the whole subject of salesmanship on paper. Describes in detail the successive steps in advertising, and how to carry them out ; how to plan the campaign, write the advertisement, get up illustrations, arrange the display, choose mediums, test and record results, systematise the advertising department. All this is based on a study of the ideas and methods of more than a hundred successful advertisers, and includes scores of tested plans and actual advertisements that have produced maximum results for them.

How Scientific Management is Applied

EXPLAINS the principles of scientific management, gives detailed descriptions of the exact methods by which it has been successfully applied, and how it can actually be operated to raise efficiency, cut costs and multiply the output of men and machines. This is the best elementary book on this new subject, and explains for the first time definitely and clearly its methods of operation, the results it will bring, and how it can be adapted to all kinds of works and conditions. Illustrated with photographs and diagrams.

How to Increase Shop Sales

188 PAGES filled with practical ideas, plans, and campaigns for increasing sales in the shop, covering every possible field for securing trade and giving the detailed methods to be used under each : how to make attractive window displays, how to conduct special sales, how to do press, poster and postal advertising, how to systematise shop-selling methods, and a dozen other avenues to a bigger business that will help to solve the retailer's selling problem.

How to Get More Out of Your Factory

CONTAINS 93 plans for cutting costs, reducing expenses and increasing output as used in actual practice. Each plan is a concrete instance of how one manufacturer actually saved money : how to get the largest return from labour, how to speed up production and get the most out of machinery and equipment, how to produce at lowest cost, how and where to look for leaks, how to prevent mistakes and waste.

How to Increase Sales

HERE is a practical and concise book that shows the salesman or manager how to direct his efforts so as to secure the largest returns. Explains the principles of salesmanship, and the definite steps and methods to be followed in making a sale. Then it shows how to handle the buyer and gain the continuing confidence of customers. Describes specific systems for carrying on all the details of selling, sales and customers records, sales management and controlling salesmen. Written out of the experience of a number of successful sales-managers and travellers in many different lines.

How to Sell More Insurance

CONTAINS 91 schemes and plans for writing more policies, tried and perfected in the field by 44 agents. Every detail of every plan is so fully given that you can put them to immediate use. For the first time in the history of insurance, the man who is actively engaged in the important work of turning prospects into policy-holders is provided with a reasoned and systematic book, which places at his disposal the accumulated experience of his fellow-workers in the field.

THE KNACK OF SELLING

A SIX-BOOK training course in salesmanship and selling methods, based on the actual experience of successful salesmen and managers. It will give the experienced business man new ideas and valuable suggestions, and it will tell the novice exactly how to go about the art of selling. The crystallised selling experience and the actual tested methods of many successful men have been here gathered together and are explained in so clear and practical a way that the reader can apply them at once. It describes the plans, methods, and ideas by which they make their sales, by which they train new men to sell and old men to sell more. These books cover the complete circle of selling : how to map out the canvas, how to get in to see the prospect, how to manage the interview, how and when to close, how to acquire the art of " mixing," how to correct your weak points. These subjects are treated in detail, and the right methods to accomplish each step in selling are pointed out in such a way as to make them applicable to any line of business.

Published as six pocket volumes, each 32 pages, 4½ inches by 8½ inches in size, bound in cloth, with covers in colours.

Price complete, 7/6 net ; postage, 6d. extra.

STANDARD BOOKS ON BUSINESS

A SERIES of independent books, covering completely the fundamental principles and operating methods of the subjects treated. These are standard works, exhaustive and authoritative, equally useful to the practical man in business and the student of commerce.

Uniformly bound in handsome dark-red cloth, stamped in gold ; 5⅜ inches by 8¾ inches in size, 200 or more pages each, printed on heavy book paper in large clear type.

Price, 5/– each net ; postage, 6d. extra.

Business Correspondence

THIS book is the most complete single-volume treatise on the subject, covering all phases of correspondence, all kinds of letters and follow-ups, as well as indexing and filing systems. It explains the principles of good correspondence ; how correspondence is most effectively used in the various departments of business, especially sales, complaints, and collections ; and the most economical method of handling departmental correspondence. It further describes general office methods for handling correspondence, and is particularly complete in its description of follow-up and filing methods with exact information adaptable to any business. Illustrated with quotations from model letters, diagrams, and system forms.

Selling Policies

HERE are the specific methods which have been successful in marketing products of all sorts at a proper selling expense. The first section explains clearly the underlying principles of salesmanship ; the second, how selling is effected in various lines ; the third, the advantages and importance of system in selling. The volume shows how to train and handle salesmen, sell by post and through the wholesaler and retailer, conduct national or local selling campaigns, increase sales and reduce selling costs. It is full of actual selling experience of successful sales managers and travellers, which will give you a clear knowledge of selling in its many phases.

Organising a Factory

CONCISELY and clearly this volume brings together the fundamental principles of works organisation and shows exactly how these can be applied in placing a manufacturing business on a profit basis. Among the points covered are :

—Necessity of system and new methods
—Organisation elements and authorities of an industrial body
—Departmental authorities, duties and responsibilities
—Accounting of expenses and costs
—How to pay labour
—How to find costs
—Depreciation of tools and its relation to cost
—Labour records and classification
—Perpetual inventories
—How to cut labour costs
—How the executive may keep in touch with the factory
—Schedules for recording factory output

In this volume the author sums up many years' experience in the application of both basic principles and time-tried specific methods for all departments of the factory. The works manager will find it helpful in evolving a smoothly running organisation and in operating his business at a profit.

Cost of Production

THIS book is one of the best elementary books on costing. It describes in a simple but practical way the prime elements that make up costs and the fundamental principles of costing. It then goes on to explain in detail the actual methods and systems to be used in carrying on a costing system and how to gather together the various elements of costs to make the total cost—labour, material, over-head, depreciation, selling expense, interest, and profit. It is illustrated with diagrams and charts showing exactly how specific costing systems in different lines of business are operated.

Buying

BUYING is most important because it is the first point at which profits may be made, and because every economy made in buying is a direct addition to profits. This volume presents fully the fundamental principles of successful purchasing as well as the detailed methods for the buyer's everyday use. It explains first the principles and methods of good buying, and secondly the systems and records to be used in carrying out buying activities. It tells how the buyer keeps in touch with his markets and sources of supply, how he keeps informed of market conditions, how he gets good prices and terms. It describes the methods to be pursued in different fields of buying —in buying for the works, buying for a retail shop, purchasing office supplies, etc. It lays out in detail the buying systems adapted to every class and size of business, illustrated with diagrams and forms which are instantly applicable.

THE LIBRARY OF BUSINESS PRACTICE

THIS work is a survey of the entire field of business method, with the object of presenting the detailed methods of every department and activity of business in such a practical and specific way that the reader can lift them out and apply them in his own work. These ten volumes are working tools for men in business, in the form of a Reference Library covering completely the entire field of business organisation and management, buying and selling, sales management and method, advertising and correspondence, accounting and costing, financing and collecting, efficiency and man-management, wholesaling and retailing, production and distribution. It constitutes the only complete practical work on BUSINESS METHODS published.

Each volume is divided into four parts, and each part deals with its specific subject completely and definitely, and at the same time links up the subject with all related lines of commercial effort. Each chapter gives detailed and specific facts and methods, with instances of how to do it and how others have done it successfully.

The 208 separate chapters of the " Library of Business Practice " have been produced with the co-operation of 173 successful men and experts in their respective lines. These men developed and used the methods which are described in the Library, and they therefore explain them in the business-like language and practical way that enable you to apply them to your own work and business.

This Library has been published in order to provide the business man with a reference work, a universal advisor and assistant, to which he can turn when he is seeking new ideas, meets a difficult situation, needs a definite method or system, wishes a broad and many-sided point of view on an important policy, seeks practical advice about any point in his work and business.

The index of the Library has been adapted to this design. It comprises 48 pages and contains over 5,000 direct references, all the most important items printed in red. The index is also laid out in a three-fold classification, so that any topic can be found without need of cross reference. Placed on the principal's desk, therefore, the Library puts the answers to the thousands of vital every-day business questions at his fingers' ends.

The "Library of Business Practice" consists of ten volumes of hard facts contained in 2,016 pages—208 separate chapters written by 173 successful business men. Each volume is printed in clear type on thin but opaque paper. The binding is a rich, red, flexible full leather, stamped in gold with gilt tops, packed in an attractive box. Price complete, £3. 15. 0. net. Postage, 8d. extra.

BUSINESS CORRESPONDENCE LIBRARY

THESE three volumes constitute a complete course in commercial correspondence, covering in detail every phase of business letter-writing and the use of letters, selling by post and mail-order methods. It forms the most exhaustive and authoritative work ever published on this subject.

The first volume explains the functions of the business letter, its plan and point of contact, and how to make letters interest, attract, and convince readers. The second volume tells the mechanics of the sales letter, how to make up lists and conduct tests, put sales schemes into letters, follow up orders and handle all classes of local trade by letter. The third volume shows how to get long-distance business by letter, how to open new fields, reach the dealer and the house salesman by post, and use the letter successfully to collect money and handle complaints. Each volume has many charts and reprints of actual letters which make graphic the various processes of correspondence.

From a study of the correspondence methods and results of hundreds of firms, it reproduces the 299 actual letters that brought the best results, with a keen analysis of the principles behind them and a description of the methods by which they were created. These include sales and advertising letters, follow-up letters to various classes of customers and dealers, letters for collecting accounts and making adjustments, and general business letters. This library is a reference work and everyday assistant that no progressive business man should fail to have in his office.

Published in three substantial volumes, 672 pages, printed on fine, heavy book paper, handsomely bound in cloth and stamped in gold. Price complete, 17/6 net ; postage, 7d. extra.

THE LIBRARY OF FACTORY MANAGEMENT

THIS six-volume Library is designed to place in the hands of works managers and manufacturers in a practical and useful form the best standardised production and management methods of to-day.

There are plenty of books filled with somebody's pet doctrines or engineering hobbies. But the Library of Factory Management gives practical and usable suggestions, proved plans and methods for immediate application, concrete ideas and hints for use in every department of the works. For this Library is practical, based wholly on the actual experience of hundreds of successful manufacturers.

Trained investigators were sent out by the publishers of this work to seek the answers to current factory problems. 1,023 of the world's most successful manufacturers gave these investigators access to the plans and policies developed by costly experience. They learned the underlying policies, they were told the everyday experience and the ingenious ideas evolved, they examined methods and practices used, they talked with managers and with workmen, they made sketches and secured hundreds of interesting photographs. They asked, in fact, the very questions you would have asked, they studied the very points you would have studied, they learned the very things that you would have wanted to learn—if you had been there yourself.

After all the material had been gathered together, it was verified and classified and edited until the best of all that these investigators had discovered about works management and making a factory pay had been crowded into these six new volumes. In this Library of Factory Management therefore is contained the united experience of 1,023 successful manufacturers who have created and operated profitable works—not only what they have done, but how they did it.

These six volumes cover the entire field of manufacturing organisation, management and operations. The methods here described will solve most problems of works production and management, machinery and equipment, construction and material, labour and costs ; for they are presented in such concrete and practical form that the reader can immediately apply their output-increasing, cost cutting, efficiency-raising and profit making plans in his own business

The Library is profusely illustrated, by means of hundreds of photographs, 144 charts and diagrams, and 99 system forms to help to make every point so clear that the reader can readily apply the methods and systems described to his own works. An index of more than 2 000 references makes it possible instantly to turn to any subject on which information is wanted

Six volumes of large size, 6 inches by 9 inches each, 1,296 pages in all, printed on fine heavy book paper, half-tones on art paper, handsomely bound in half-leather, stamped in gold, contained in an attractive box.

Price complete, £3. 15. o. net; postage, 9d. extra.

The Automatic Letter-writer

THE Automatic LetterWriter is really not a book at all, but just what its name implies—a *mechanical correspondent*. It consists of a large volume containing hundreds of numbered paragraphs, carefully classified, indexed, and arranged for instant reference and use. They cover every phase of business routine — selling, dispatching, complaints, collections, inquiries, and requests for information; and they have been selected after a careful study of the actual correspondence and letter requirements of hundreds of firms. The paragraphs are printed in typewriter type of standard letter width, so that you see at a glance how much space each will occupy.

All you have to do in dealing with an inquiry, answering a complaint, writing a sales letter, or giving desired information, is to turn to " The Automatic Letter-Writer " and write the numbers of the appropriate paragraphs on the margin of the letter: the typist does the rest. The system of classification and annotation is so flexible that thousands of different combinations can be introduced—giving the note of personal attention to all your letters. In addition to the assortment of tested paragraphs, nearly 100 actual standard letters and follow-ups are reproduced in full.

The volume also contains chapters on how to organise the correspondence work, how to answer correspondence by form letters, and how to reduce the cost of letter-writing all the way through from the opening of the post in the morning to its dispatch in the evening. This volume can either be used independently or as supplementary in connection with the Business Correspondence Library.

A large octavo volume, size $7\frac{1}{2}$ inches by $10\frac{5}{10}$ inches, 192 pages, printed on heavy strong paper, with a unique thumb index, bound in durable cloth, gold stamped.

Price, 10/6 net; postage, 6d. extra.

SYSTEM—THE MAGAZINE OF BUSINESS

SYSTEM, the pre-eminent Business Magazine, describes practical ways for organising every item of the day's work and every branch of a business, thus enabling one to do more in the same time with far less labour, less worry, and more profit. The purpose of SYSTEM is to seek out for its readers the most successful methods and systems in actual use to-day, and so describe their operations and principles that they can make direct use of them in their business and adapt them to their own work.

Big enough so that it can adequately cover the whole field of business, SYSTEM describes every month latest methods and devices that save time and labour, cut costs and reduce expenses. It tells the plans that have actually increased output, raised efficiency, and built up bigger businesses. It explains the latest methods for advertising and selling, finding new markets, and getting more trade.

SYSTEM has been endorsed by prominent business men the world over, because the ideas, methods and plans it describes are not theory ; they are practical, drawn from the actual experience of successful business men in all branches of business. Therefore every idea and method described can be lifted from the Magazine and immediately applied by the reader.

Whatever business you are in, whatever position you hold, SYSTEM will help you to do more and to make more. No situation will find you unprepared if you make use of what SYSTEM brings you each month. Every issue of the Magazine is full of business suggestions for you, ready and waiting to be applied to your own work and business.

SYSTEM is 1/- per copy from your bookseller or newsagent. The annual subscription price is 12/- per year, twelve complete monthly issues, carriage pre-paid.

JOHN KEY & SONS, LTD., Clothiers, Rugeley—"The writer would not willingly miss even one number of the Magazine, which is kept on file for reference, the various articles being indexed and cross-indexed on cards."

T. PINK & SONS, LTD., Portsmouth—Time after time I have used ideas described in *System* with great profit to my own Company. Anyone reading the Magazine in an intelligent manner should be able to gain information of general principles which are applicable to any kind of business."

HOW YOU CAN GET THE BOOKS YOU WANT

YOU can obtain any of the business books in this list at once either at your booksellers or from the publishers direct. Many of these books your bookseller will carry in stock. the others he can get for you by return of post.

—Tick off the books you want on the list below and ask your bookseller for them.

—Or send the list to the publishers with your own name and address and the name of your bookseller, and the books will at once be forwarded to him for delivery to you.

—Or if you wish the books sent to you direct by the publishers, enclose remittance at the listed price, plus the carriage charge, Postage on orders from abroad extra.

List for Ordering Books Published by

A. W. SHAW CO., Ltd., 43, Shoe Lane, LONDON, E.C.

—How to Organise a Business	2/6 net ; postage, 3d. extra
—How to Write Letters that Win	2/6 net ; postage, 3d. extra
—How to Run a Shop at a Profit	2/6 net ; postage, 3d. extra
—How to Write Advertisements	2/6 net ; postage, 3d. extra
—How to Increase Sales	2/6 net ; postage, 3d. extra
—How Scientific Management is Applied	2/6 net ; postage, 3d. extra
—How to Increase Shop Sales	2/6 net ; postage, 3d. extra
—How to Systematise Your Factory	2/6 net ; postage, 3d. extra
—How to Get More out of Your Factory	2/6 net ; postage, 3d. extra
—How to Sell More Insurance	2/6 net ; postage 3d. extra
—Business Correspondence	5/- net ; postage, 6d. extra
—Selling Policies..	5/- net ; postage, 6d. extra
—Organising a Factory	5/- net ; postage, 6d. extra
—Cost of Production	5/- net ; postage, 6d. extra
—Buying	5/- net ; postage, 6d. extra
—The Knack of Selling—6 pocket volumes	7/6 complete ; postage, 6d. extra
—Business Correspondence Library—3 volumes	17/6 complete ; postage, /d. extra
—Automatic Letter Writer	10/6 each net ; postage, 6d. extra
—Library of Business Practice—10 volumes	£3 15 0 complete ; postage, 8d. extra
—Library of Factory Management—6 volumes	£3 15 0 complete ; postage, 9d. extra
—SYSTEM, The Magazine of Business	1/- per copy ; 12/- Annual

Subscription in the United Kingdom, 14/6 abroad.

12

Printed in Great Britain
by Amazon

31405817R00089